"Ninety years ago, Albert Schweitzer recognized that Paul was the first Christian mystic. Now, Harvey Egan has expanded and deepened the picture of Paul the mystic in this new and penetrating series, investigating the apostolic, christological, Trinitarian, and ecclesiological dimensions of the mysticism of the Apostle to the Gentiles. All subsequent Christian mystics read and cited Paul, but Egan's work shows how much Pauline themes were, indeed, foundational for later Christian mysticism. By considering Paul's relation both to previous Jewish traditions, as well as to subsequent Christian history, Egan's incisive work casts light both on the origins and the later story of Christian mysticism. A ground-breaking series for biblical scholars, as well as for students of mysticism."

—Bernard McGinn, University of Chicago

"Harvey D. Egan, SJ, brings years of study and writing on the Christian mystical tradition to this rich exploration of one of the foundational sources of that tradition: Paul, apostle and mystic. Though rooted in the faith of Israel, Paul's mysticism is his transformative consciousness of the fulfillment of God's salvific plan in the crucified and risen Jesus Christ. Paul's mystical consciousness animated his apostolic conviction that fulfillment in Christ is good news not only for Israel, but for all peoples, indeed for the whole of creation."

—Robert P. Imbelli, author *of Rekindling the Christic Imagination*

"Father Harvey Egan is a former doctoral student of Karl Rahner, an expert in Christian mysticism, and is adept in New Testament scholarship. After reading all of his books and many of his articles over the last thirty-five years, I can vouch that in this vibrant and insightful book he will be the best guide for those desirous of understanding St. Paul's mystical consciousness as well as the real nature of Christian mysticism."

—Louis Roy, OP, Dominican University College, Ottawa

"I can think of no better guide to the Christian mystical tradition than Fr. Harvey Egan, SJ. Learned, prayerful, articulate, inviting, and always accessible, he is among the best of teachers."

—James Martin, SJ, author of *Jesus: A Pilgrimage*

"Harvey Egan has been engaged with Christian mystical traditions for much of his scholarly life. He now brings his careful scholarship and vast knowledge to a surprisingly neglected field—the mystical consciousness of the Apostle Paul recorded in his letters. Professor Egan is uniquely able to assess and interpret Paul's enigmatic references to his mystical experience and to show its relevance for Christians today."

—**Richard Clifford**, SJ, Boston College School of Theology and Ministry

"I loved this book both for its emphasis on the experience Paul had on the road to Damascus as well as his urgent drive to preach the real truth that Jesus is the Risen Lord. The reader will enjoy a double gift: a solid understanding of Christian mysticism flowing from Trinitarian mystery and Paul's expression of that mystery in the corpus he left to the church. I highly recommend this book, which is the fruit of fifty years of study and prayer."

—**Lawrence S. Cunningham**, University of Notre Dame

"Through keen insights into the profound mystical transformation which incorporation into Christ and his mystical body brings, Father Egan is able to explore and unveil the mystical dimensions, primarily, of St. Paul and of St. Ignatius of Loyola, perhaps the two paradigmatic mystics in action, along with some others, each reflecting and lighting up the others. A welcome, challenging, even provocative, study!"

—**William Thompson-Uberuaga**, emeritus professor, Duquesne University

"Professor Emeritus Harvey Egan, SJ, a premier scholar of Christian mysticism, guides the reader on an inspiring journey into biblical theology that first clarifies and illuminates the meaning of Christian mysticism, then convincingly argues that Paul is 'Christianity's premier apostolic mystic.' Egan's series, aimed at educated laity as well as clergy and students of Christian mysticism, fills a yawning need for an authoritative, orthodox understanding of mysticism as lived by Christianity's foremost apostolic author. Along the way, Egan rescues heaven for spiritual theology by joining heaven and earth, thereby giving heaven earthly purchase in the vocabulary of Christian discipleship, as the incarnation of God in Jesus-Messiah fulfills Isaiah 65:17: 'See, I am creating new heavens and a new earth.' Moreover, few biblical-theological books evoke rich sociopolitical application that readers will find here."

—**David G. Schultenover**, SJ, professor emeritus, Marquette University

Paul: Christianity's Premier Apostolic Mystic

Paul: Christianity's Premier Apostolic Mystic

Harvey D. Egan, SJ

FOREWORD BY
Michael A. Fahey, SJ

CASCADE *Books* · Eugene, Oregon

PAUL: CHRISTIANITY'S PREMIER APOSTOLIC MYSTIC

Cascade Books
An Imprint of Wipf and Stock Publishers
199 W. 8th Ave., Suite 3
Eugene, OR 97401

www.wipfandstock.com

PAPERBACK ISBN: 978-1-7252-9151-5
HARDCOVER ISBN: 978-1-7252-9150-8
EBOOK ISBN: 978-1-7252-9152-2

Cataloguing-in-Publication data:

Names: Egan, Harvey D., author. | Fahey, Michael A., foreword.

Title: Paul: Christianity's premier apostolic mystic / by Harvey D. Egan ; foreword by Michael A. Fahey.

Description: Eugene, OR: Cascade Books, 2021 | Includes bibliographical references.

Identifiers: ISBN 978-1-7252-9151-5 (paperback) | ISBN 978-1-7252-9150-8 (hardcover) | ISBN 978-1-7252-9152-2 (ebook)

Subjects: LCSH: Paul, the Apostle, Saint. | Bible.—Epistles of Paul—Criticism, interpretation, etc.| Mysticism. | Church history—ca. 30–100.

Classification: BS2506.3 E33 2021 (print) | BS2506.3 (ebook)

Dedicated to:
These holy and extraordinary scholars
who have so influenced my Jesuit life and apostolate:

Frederick C. Copleston, SJ
Michael A. Fahey, SJ
Joseph A. Fitzmyer, SJ
Bernard J. F. Lonergan, SJ
Bernard McGinn
Karl Rahner, SJ
Nicholas Thomas Wright

Contents

Foreword

I APPRECIATE THE AUTHOR'S invitation to compose a foreword to this volume. My first contact with the epistles of Paul of Tarsus was, as an altar boy, hearing passages read out loud hurriedly in Latin by a presiding priest at Mass. I understood next to nothing. Then, for my birthday, I received a handsome bilingual missal with an English translation that made reading in advance possible. In the early 1950s in the Jesuit novitiate, our emphasis was largely on the four Gospels combined into a single synopsis with no heed to redaction criticism. During our month-long experience of Ignatius of Loyola's *Spiritual Exercises*, Pauline perspectives were not obvious.

Years later in the 1960s I began full-time study of Scripture and theology. I remember how difficult I found understanding the Letter to the Romans (RSV translation). I read it over and over, eventually relying on the French *Bible de Jérusalem*, which organized the letter with headings and footnotes. Much still eluded me. I made a tape recording of the epistle, often listening in search of fuller comprehension. My progress was still modest.

In the ensuing years, the number of New Testament commentaries increased: weighty series, numerous scholarly articles summarized in *New Testament Abstracts*, parish-level companions. But other interests beckoned to me: historical exegesis, hermeneutics, and reader response. My attention to Paul regrettably waned.

Professor Harvey Egan's original and holistic presentation of St. Paul's transformative experience of meeting the risen Christ on the road to Damascus, his apostolic mysticism, and his expatiations of Jesus' sometimes concise teachings has enkindled in me a renewed interest and comprehension of this pioneer missionary's convictions. I anticipate that many other readers will experience this exciting sense of discovery.

Each week from the postal service or directly online I receive advertisements from publishing houses often announcing a new study of St. Paul's epistles. Why, you might ask, yet one more book on that topic, such as Egan's? I maintain that his study explores new territory because it approaches the texts by interpreting them in light of his decades of research on the nature of mysticism. In turn, he blends that with his extensive knowledge of Karl Rahner's doctrinal theology. Likewise, he continues to consult exegetical writings of experts such as N. T. Wright and the late Joseph Fitzmyer (one of his former teachers). *De Paulo numquam satis.*

Not long ago, in reviewing a new book on ecclesiology by an Irish theologian, I suggested to future readers that they start first with the last chapter. Here, with Egan's book, I make a similar proposal, namely to begin with the sixth and last chapter on the meaning of Pauline "new creation." In outlining the stunning conclusion he appropriates the sadly neglected implications of the terse creedal affirmation "I believe in the resurrection of the dead." What is it that comes afterwards for both human and non-human creation? Not the end, but the *beginning.* "No eye has seen, no ear has heard, and no mind has imagined . . ." (1 Cor 2:9).

Dr. theol. Michael A. Fahey, SJ

Emmett Doerr Professor Emeritus, Marquette University
Weston, Massachusetts

Acknowledgements

I WISH TO THANK my friend and colleague Michael A. Fahey, SJ Emmett Doerr Professor Emeritus, Marquette University, Sister Mary Augustine, lsp, David G. Schultenover, SJ, Professor Emeritus, Marquette University, and Revd Dr Robin Parry, editor, and Cascade Books for their suggestions and corrections. Of course, any errors are mine.

Introduction

"[Paul's] letters contain some things that are
hard to understand . . ." (2 Pet 3:16)

MY INTEREST IN THE Christian mystics began in 1959 when I was an electrical engineering student at Worcester Polytechnic Institute and read my first mystical text, St. John of the Cross' *Dark Night of the Soul*. The book stirred me deeply and I never lost my initial conviction that John of the Cross and other mystics of the Christian tradition are of immense importance to anyone interested in living a deeper Christian life.

My 1960 entrance into the Society of Jesus further intensified my fascination with the mystics. Within two months I had completed Ignatius' thirty-day retreat and experienced firsthand the healing and transforming power of his famous *Spiritual Exercises*. Despite my enthusiasm for the *Exercises*, my reading list did not include anything by or about St. Ignatius of Loyola. My master of novices, Father Thomas G. O'Callaghan asked: What do you have against Ignatius? His ironic question was one of the great graces of my life. I had nothing against Ignatius, but simply needed guidance.

In 1969 I traveled to Germany to begin theological studies as one of Karl Rahner's doctoral students. My dissertation attempted to translate the mystical wisdom of St. Ignatius of Loyola's *Spiritual Exercises* into a contemporary framework by using Rahner's transcendental method, which culminated in my 1987 book, *Ignatius Loyola the Mystic*. It argued that popular and even scholarly emphasis on Ignatius' apostolic successes as well as a mistaken view of him as a reformer, an ascetic, and an advocate of discursive, methodical prayer have obscured Ignatius the apostolic *mystic*.

1

Throughout my Jesuit studies from 1962 to 1969, I read many anthologies of the Christian mystics.[1] In 1975 I began teaching at Boston College, taught courses on Christian mysticism, and published a small book, *What Are They Saying about Mysticism*, then *Christian Mysticism: The Future of a Tradition*, followed by *An Anthology of Christian Mysticism*, later *Soundings in the Christian Mystical Tradition*, and recently, in conjunction with Father Joseph H. Wong, OSB Cam, *The Christology and Mystical Theology of Karl Rahner*. I owe much to the definitive multi-volume works of the premier scholar of the Western mystical tradition, the University of Chicago Professor Emeritus Bernard McGinn.

During my theological studies at the "old Woodstock" in Maryland, I was blessed to have the extraordinary professor and world-class scholar on the apostle Paul, Father Joseph Fitzmyer, SJ. He published the Anchor Bible Commentary on 1 Corinthians when in his nineties. Later on, the monumental works of the British scripture scholar N. T. Wright and his dialogue partners only deepened my profound fascination with St. Paul, Christianity's premier apostolic mystic.

Unlike the other apostles, Paul had not lived with Jesus for three years. Nevertheless, because of his encounter with the risen Jesus on the Damascus road, his felt-knowledge of mystery of God in Christ made him not only an apostle but also Christianity's earliest apostolic mystic and a mystical theologian par excellence. I mean by a Christian mystic someone who is explicitly and directly conscious of the immediate or direct presence of the Trinity and/or Christ. I understand mystical experience not only as discrete, individual experiences but also as experience in the sense that an experienced musician instinctively knows and loves music. Thus, I prefer to speak of mystical consciousness and the mystical life. In other words, this present book focuses on Paul's mystical worldview, his mystical horizon, the lens through which he comprehended that God consummated Israel's history through the sending of Jesus-Messiah[2] and the Holy Spirit. In fact, one reason why Paul's epistles often make for such difficult reading is that he was rethinking the Jewish Scriptures in terms of Jesus-Messiah and the Holy Spirit. This zealous Jewish Pharisee grew to understand Jesus-Messiah as Judaism fulfilled and perfected.

---

1. The best anthology to date is McGinn, *Essential Writings*.

2. N. T. Wright frequently uses the term Jesus-Messiah because it is closer to original meaning of Christ, the anointed one, the Messiah. It underscores Jesus' Jewishness, which the Enlightenment attempted to cover up. See John 1:41.

A theological tradition, beginning in earnest with Thomas Aquinas and enduring almost to the present day, attributed to the proto-man Adam and Moses the highest degree of mystical consciousness possible in this life. This tradition argues that if that were true for Old Testament figures, then it must also be true of St. Paul in the New Testament. One of the earliest usages of the word *mystical* referred to how Jesus-Messiah is revealed in the Jewish scriptures.[3] Did not Jesus say to the Emmaus disciples: "How foolish you are, and how slow to believe all that the prophets have spoken! And beginning with Moses and all the prophets, he explained to them what was said in all the scriptures concerning himself" (Luke 24:24).

I maintain that the light from the face of the risen Christ, whom Paul encountered on the Damascus road, and what he wrote about this light in 2 Corinthians 4:6 ("For God, who said, 'Let light shine out of darkness,' made his light shine in our hearts to give us the light of the knowledge of God's glory displayed in the face of Christ") is the mystical light in which Paul wrote his letters and saw his call to be Jesus-Messiah's apostle.

Although Paul clearly had mystical experiences in the sense of distinct, transitory, transformative events, the term *experience* lends itself to a misunderstanding of mysticism as particular feelings or sensible perceptions that are too easily separated from understanding, judging, deciding, and loving—that which forms the full range of the human person as a self-conscious and free subject. Thus, I claim that Paul's mysticism—as in all genuine Christian mysticism—became the center of his life, which engendered in him new ways of knowing and loving that also involved a transformative decision about how he would live. His mystical worldview was nothing less than the triune God and/or Jesus-Messiah, which was the horizon against which Paul's knew, comprehended, and loved everything else. One might say that the Jewish *Shema*, "Hear, O Israel: the LORD our God, the LORD is one"—but rethought in the light of Jesus-Messiah and the Holy Spirit—was what Paul ultimately experienced in *all* his experience, what was ultimately understood in *all* his understanding, what was ultimately judged in *all* his judgments, and what was ultimately decided upon in *all* his decisions.

I regard Paul as the world's greatest missionary, one whom scholars estimate walked over fifteen hundred miles to plant the flag of the Lord Jesus in Roman colonies where Caesar was supposedly lord. And I would

---

3. For the classic work on the history of the word *mysticism*, see, Bouyer, "Mysticism," 42–55.

3

emphasize Paul's numerous and dangerous trips by ship. In his duties as God's messenger, the Lukan Paul is sent specifically to the synagogues of the Roman world. When Paul was first converted, for example, he immediately entered the synagogues in order to report that Jesus is "God's Son" (Acts 9:20). This regular engagement in the synagogues prevailed throughout Paul's career, becoming what Luke called his "custom" (Acts 17:2). Everywhere Paul went, so it seems in Luke's account, he went first to the synagogue—not to the idolatrous temples nor the pagan forums. There, in the synagogues, he found receptive ears among Jews and God-fearing gentiles (Acts 13:5–14; 14:1; 16:13–14; 17:2–17; 18:19; 19:8). I suggest that one google a map that illustrates Paul's journeys, which makes for fascinating study.

Paul's mystical charism also revealed itself in other ways. Acts of healing and exorcisms went hand-in-hand with his apostolic ministry. For example, "God did extraordinary miracles through Paul, so that even handkerchiefs and aprons that had touched him were taken to the sick, and their illnesses were cured and the evil spirits left them. Some Jews who went around driving out evil spirits tried to invoke the name of the Lord Jesus over those who were demon-possessed. They would say, 'In the name of the Jesus whom Paul preaches, I command you to come out'" (Acts 19:1–13). This indicates that Paul was well-known both as a Spirit-filled healer and an exorcist. Like his Master, Paul made the lame walk (Acts 14:8–10), raised the dead (Acts 20:11–12), cured the fevered (Acts 28:8), and healed various other ailments (Acts 19:11–12; 28:9). He proved himself to be a capable discerner of both healing-signs and of plague-signs, as when he blinded his prophetic opponent Elymas, the magician (Acts 13:12).

It should be pointed out that according to Luke's account of Paul's ministry, neither letter-writing nor theological exposition were central to the apostle's career.[4] The Lukan Paul, as a matter of fact, was not much of a thinker at all. Rather, he was primarily a doer: a wonderworker, a messenger, and a seer. These seemingly forgotten modes of Paul's ministry, I would maintain, in large part defined the apostle's character long before his epistles were collected and meticulously scrutinized by churchmen and academics alike. While these letters are undoubtedly the product of a powerful mystical mind, their theological reflection represent a mere snapshot of the apostle's

4. For the tension between what Paul related about himself in his epistles and what Luke wrote about him in Acts, see, Wright and Bird, *The New Testament in Its World*, 347–49. For the most part, what I have written avoids the controversy.

output. The Paul of history, unlike the Paul of the church and the academy, was, in the first place, a man of startling *deeds*, a man with a message from God, and a man guided by ecstatic encounters with the divine. In short, he was Christianity's premier apostolic mystic.

As someone who has spent many years studying and praying over Paul's writings, I resonate with what St. John Chrysostom wrote about him:

> As I keep hearing the Epistles of the blessed Paul read . . . whenever we are celebrating the memorials of the holy martyrs, gladly do I enjoy the spiritual trumpet, and get stirred and warmed with desire at recognizing the voice so dear to me, and seem to fancy him all but present to my sight, and behold him conversing with me. But I grieve and am pained, that all people do not know this man, as much as they ought to know him; but some are so far ignorant of him, as not even to know for certainty the number of his Epistles. And this comes not of incapacity, but of their not wishing to be continually conversing with this blessed man. For it is not through any natural readiness and sharpness of wit that even I am acquainted with as much as I do know, if I do know anything, but only to a continual cleaving to this man, and an earnest affection towards him.[5]

Martin Luther considered justification by faith alone to be Paul's central teaching—a view that has endured in some quarters to the present day. However, what Paul wrote in the first chapter of his Epistle to the Romans proclaims otherwise: "Paul, a servant of Christ Jesus, called to be an apostle and set apart for the gospel of God—the gospel he promised beforehand through his prophets in the holy scriptures regarding his Son, who as to his earthly life was a descendant of David, and who through the Spirit of holiness was appointed the Son of God in power by his resurrection from the dead: Jesus Christ our Lord." Thus, Paul understood the gospel as centering on the bodily resurrection of Jesus-Messiah who explicitly designated Paul as an apostle to preach this gospel. This has nothing to do with the later faith-works Reformation controversy. And, in Paul's way of thinking, faith is the response of the whole person to this entire gospel. It is both the faith *through which* one believes and the faith *that* one believes.

Moreover, given the contemporary popular and even scholarly skewed opinions on what constitutes Christian mysticism and the often contentious contemporary approaches to the apostle Paul, I plan to explain what

5. Chrys. *Praef. Hom. Rom.*, quoted in Wright and Bird, *The New Testament and Its World*, 337.

authentic Christian mysticism really is and why the term *apostolic mystic* is an appropriate designation for the apostle Paul. I concede that the fairly recent and contemporary prodigious work on both Christian mysticism and also the apostle Paul has made this book rather difficult.

Yet, no one has produced anything substantial on the apostolic mystic Paul since Albert Schweitzer's now outdated 1931 volume. I am also keenly aware of what one reads in 2 Peter 3:16: "There are some things in [Paul's letters] hard to understand, which the ignorant and unstable twist to their own destruction, as they do the other scriptures." So, within a generation, people were grumbling that Paul was sometimes hard to understand and some were taking him the wrong way. All the same, it is no accident that many of the great moments in church history—think of Augustine, Aquinas, Luther, Barth—have come about through fresh engagement with Paul's work.

When asked why Paul, with only seventy or eighty pages of text to his name in the average Bible, has been more widely read and had far greater influence than the other great letter writers of antiquity—for example, Cicero or Seneca—and for that matter the great public intellectuals and founders of the movements of his day and ours, the answer is clear: it is his *range of writing*, from the urgent to the appealing, from the prophetic to the poetic, and from intellectual rigor to passionate advocacy. The man who could write Philemon and Romans side-by-side was a man for every occasion.

What transformed Saul the zealous Pharisee into St. Paul the apostolic mystic? Who, apart from Jesus-Messiah, was more formative for recasting the Jewish worldview around messianic hopes and establishing kingdom-centered Christian communities in the West than Paul? Who, apart from maybe Peter, was more influential in founding churches across the Roman empire—communities that were distinguished by their devotion to the Lord Jesus (not Caesar) and committed to a radically countercultural way of life—than Paul? Who, apart from maybe Irenaeus, was more formidable when it came to defending the gospel against being diluted and adulterated by dissident groups than Paul? Who has written some of the world's masterpieces on Jesus-Messiah, love, and other topics? Paul! Who was Christianity's premier apostolic mystic? Again, the apostle Paul!

What was Paul trying to do? What made him do it? Why did he keep on going back to the synagogue, even though this got him beaten time and time again? Why did he continue with his message on the gentiles, even though his fellow Jews and pagans alike thought that he was a crazy Jew and wanted to run him out of town? Why did he carry on relentlessly, with his apparent desire to be in several places at once, to write to five churches at once, to explain and to cajole, to teach and to proclaim, to travel and travel and travel some more? And on one occasion he became so drained of energy that he claimed to have despaired of life itself. What was it that eventually regenerated his faith and hope? What assessment can we make of his brilliant mind and passionate heart? Why did the movement he started, against all odds, become in a fairly short time the church we see in the fourth and fifth centuries? What was it about this busy, volatile man, that, despite everything, seems to have been so effective.

Paul always emphasized Jesus-Messiah as the shocking fulfillment of Israel's hopes. As a genuinely human being, Jesus was nothing less than the true image and embodiment of Israel's God. In addition, without leaving Jewish monotheism, Paul and his Jesus followers worshipped and invoked Jesus as Lord and the Holy Spirit *within*, not alongside, the service of the living and true God. Jesus was the definitive reason why all idols, all rival lords, should be forsaken. In all history, only Paul ever wrote that, compared to Jesus, all else can be considered pure excrement.

Jesus was not only Paul's *starting point* but also his *goal*. He never wavered in his conviction that Jesus would descend from heaven, which is not in the sky, but is rather God's dimension of present reality. Jesus would come from heaven to earth in order to complete the already begun task of filling earth with the life of heaven, God's sphere. God's plan had always been to unite all things in heaven and on earth in the ultimate temple, Jesus-Messiah and his Holy Spirit.

Paul believed that Israel's God, having abandoned the temple at the time of the Babylonian exile and never having fulfilled his promise to return in his invisible and powerful glory, had suddenly, shockingly, and disruptively revealed himself in Jesus-Messiah, breaking in upon an unready world and an unready people. He believed in the new creation, a coming great transformation that would take place at Jesus' return or his reappearing, the time when heaven and earth would come together at last. This explains both Paul's identity and why he succeeded. He not only advocated but also made possible through his person and writings a new way of life, a new kind of community. Because of the gospel, the good news of Jesus-Messiah, the old barriers between Jew and Greek, master and slave, male and female—I would add also between people of all colors and races—were to be abolished in Jesus-Messiah.

It was also because in Jesus-Messiah the promises of Psalm 2 had come true—that God would set his anointed king over the rulers of the nations. That means that Paul's work must be regarded just as much as social and political as it is theological and religious. Every time Paul expounded justification, it formed part of his argument that in Jesus-Messiah there was a single family composed of believing Jews and believing gentiles, master and slave, male and female—a family that demonstrated to the world that there was a new way of being human.

One should also notice how Paul stressed and even celebrated the sufferings that he and others would indeed endure because of their loyalty to Jesus. He pioneered the idea of a *suffering* apostleship through which the message of the crucified Jesus would not only be displayed, but also be effective in the world. This is about a new kind of community and a new kind of politics.

Paul introduced as well a new and demanding way of behaving that in the ancient world was nonsense to pagan sensibilities but good news for many—especially women, the poor, ethnic minorities, slaves, and children—those who were the most vulnerable to the normal patterns of pagan behavior. Galen, the famous second-century Greek physician, surgeon, and philosopher, observed that the followers of this strange new cult appear to be senseless. Not only were they chaste, but they also believed in bodily resurrection. Pagans routinely practiced infanticide for unwanted children in general and girls in particular—common even in our age—but the Christians followed the Jewish views in renouncing such behavior. Moreover, contrary to the opinions of many contemporary Bible readers, the fresh evaluation of the role of women, though it came ultimately from Jesus himself, was mediated not least through Paul. One should be aware of the fact that Paul listed several women among his colleagues and fellow workers—including possibly one apostle, Junia—and also entrusted Phoebe with the responsibility of delivering and almost certainly expounding his Epistle to the Romans.

Paul's communities were essentially outward looking, and became rapidly known for their charitable works. Within a few generations, Christians established hospitals and cared for all—not only the upper classes, as the pagans did. Education in the ancient world was almost exclusively for an elite. Christians, however, valued education, particularly reading, regardless of class. Paul's vision of a united and holy community, prayerful, rooted in the scriptural story of ancient Israel, facing social and political hostility, but insisting on doing good to all people, especially the poor, would always be central. His intellectual vision of the one God was reshaped not only around Jesus and the Holy Spirit but also challenged the views of the wider world of philosophy.

Concerning Paul's direct authorship of the entire Pauline corpus, there continues ongoing discussions. I do not address this issue for the following reason: even if Paul may not have directly dictated every one of the epistles, their content certainly reflects an accurate expression of his convictions.[6] As a consequence, this book will argue that Paul's mysticism and apostolic life are two sides of the same coin. Not to recognize him as Christianity's premier apostolic mystic is to fail to comprehend his heart and soul—the driving force for everything he did.

---

6. Wright and Bird, *The New Testament in Its World*, 528–43 and the introduction to each epistle for more information on this difficult topic.

Chapter 1

From Saul, the Zealous Pharisee, to Paul, the Zealous Apostolic Mystic

Saul, the Zealous Pharisee

"As to zeal, a persecutor of the church." (Phil 3:6)

IN PAUL'S CLASHES WITH the Judaizers, namely Jewish Christians who insisted that the gentile Christians be circumcised and observe the Jewish law, Paul proclaimed both harshly and ironically in Philippians 3:4-6:

> Watch out for those dogs, those evildoers, those mutilators of the flesh. For it is we who are the circumcision, we who serve God by his Spirit, who boast in Christ Jesus, and who put no confidence in the flesh—though I myself have reasons for such confidence. If someone else thinks they have reasons to put confidence in the flesh, I have more: circumcised on the eighth day, of the people of Israel, of the tribe of Benjamin, a Hebrew of Hebrews; in regard to the law, a Pharisee; as for zeal, persecuting the church; as for righteousness based on the law.

This text reveals four salient aspects of Saul's identity before he became the apostle Paul, Christianity's premier apostolic mystic: thoroughly Jewish, faultless in regard to the Torah; his most regrettable sin: he persecuted and tried to destroy the church of God; and zeal, a code word for an often-violent Pharisee. The text also indirectly suggests—which Paul later explicated—that "a person is not a Jew who is one only outwardly, nor is circumcision merely outward and physical. No, a person is a Jew who is one inwardly; and circumcision is circumcision of the heart, by the Spirit, not by the written code" (Rom 2:28–29).

The Diaspora Jew Saul of Tarsus was probably born a few years after Jesus, perhaps as late as 10 AD. Tarsus was the capital of Cilicia in Asia Minor—present-day Turkey, plus other lands—and a strategic military center for Rome's campaigns east of the Euphrates. Taken over in Alexander the Great's fourth conquest of the East, Pompeii later annexed it for Rome in 63 B.C. During the reign of Emperor Augustus, when Saul was born, Tarsus grew to a population of about half a million people. It surpassed both Athens and Alexandria as a seat of learning and became known especially for its poets and for its schools of philosophy and rhetoric.

The evangelist Luke wrote that Saul was a Roman citizen by birth. His grandfather or father may have settled in Tarsus, where there was a significant Jewish community. Thus, Saul was raised in a Romanized Hellenistic city, in an urban Jewish family, involved in Diaspora Jewish life, and undoubtedly among the artisan class. As quoted earlier, Saul-Paul underscored his ethnic and religious heritage as a Jew. Greek was certainly his first language, although he knew the Hebrew scriptures intimately, as well as the Septuagint, the Greek version of the Jewish scriptures. He had been exposed to Greco-Roman literature, rhetoric, culture, and philosophy in both the city in general and his education in particular. Probably in Saul's teens, he left Tarsus and trained in the Pharisaic traditions in Jerusalem. In the many ongoing debates about what it meant to be a loyal Jew, all the evidence suggests that he allied himself with the more politically militant and religiously zealous Shammaite wing.

Popular opinion incorrectly views the Judaism of Saul's day as a religion of legalistic works righteousness, that is, earning one's way to God by one's own efforts ("works," in Luther's pejorative sense), an historical error that continues to this day. However, recent scholarship has convincingly shown that because God took the initiative in making a covenant with his chosen people, God's grace preceded everything they did.[1] The Jews kept the law out of gratitude; not to enter God's chosen people, but to show that they were already there. Thus, keeping the Jewish law—in its full form—was the human grateful response to God's covenantal initiative, not "works." It was definitely not the old Pelagian heresy according to which humans must pull themselves up by their own moral bootstraps and therefore earn justification and salvation. The Jews kept the law not in order to *get into* the covenant people but to *stay in them*—and as a mark

---

1. Boccaccini and Segovia, *Paul the Jew.*

of their being God's chosen people. Neither was theirs the mistaken view that one must keep the law "to get into heaven."

The Pharisaic worldview centered on monotheism, election, and eschatology, that is, one God, one people of God, and one future of God's world. The *Shema* was a personal statement of allegiance to this one God in particular. To pray, "O Israel, Yhwh our God, Yhwh is one," stiffened resistance to persecution and summoned up courage for martyrdom. For example, in 2 Maccabees, the mother of seven sons strengthened the resolve of her youngest son by appealing to the God who created from nothing and who raised the dead bodily. She used these views in the service of political resistance. That is what Pharisaic monotheism looked like.

The Pharisees and certainly other Jews viewed Israel as chosen by Yhwh to be the people through whom the Creator would remedy the world's evils. However, what happens when Israel itself becomes skewed and evil? The Pharisees' answer was clear: Israel needed to learn how to keep the Torah properly. A hardline Pharisee might well say that it was not enough to keep the biblical laws, which separated them from the nations. They must also keep the oral laws that bring the Torah into everyday life. This would separate them from compromised Jews. The early Christians—and Paul himself—saw a different answer: the crucified and risen Jesus-Messiah.

Thus, the Pharisees made sharp distinctions between themselves and a large multitude of Jews, whom they regarded as compromised, assimilated, or otherwise insufficiently serious in their Torah practice. So, a line was drawn not only between Jews and gentiles but also within the company of Jews themselves. For this reason, Saul would have grown up in a world of fierce debate and party loyalty. The key issue at stake between the more lenient Hillelites and the stricter Shammaite interpreters of the law was not just a matter of private or personal piety. The burning issue was as much political as it was theological. It was about Israel's aims and agenda: for the people, the land, and the temple.

The Hillelites pursued a policy of live and let live. As long as they were allowed to study and practice the Jewish law in peace, then let the pseudo-king Herod, the Roman Pontius Pilate, and even the corrupt high priest Caiaphas rule by not causing unrest! Because the Shammaites believed that many Jews had made serious compromises with paganism, they rejected the Hillelites' views as not good enough. In the Shammaite view, the Torah itself demanded that Israel be free from gentile oppression, unrestricted in its service of God, and they forbade the calling of anyone master or lord except the one true God himself.

For some first-century Jews, zeal was something you did with a knife—violence. They longed for revolution against Rome and looked back to their heroes in the book of Maccabees. For example, the priest Mattathias, who so burned with zeal that he killed the Jew and the pagan officer beside him who were about to offer pagan sacrifice in full public view, and then tore down the pagan altar; the priest Phinehas who thrust a javelin through an Israelite man and into the stomach of his Midianite mistress while they were together in the man's tent; and the prophet Elijah who killed the Canaanite prophets of the pagan God Baal after an amusing display of miraculous power—these were the Shammaites' exemplars.

There was more to zeal than fervent prayer and self-righteous religiosity. Bent on revolutionary zeal for God and the Torah, the extreme Shammaites were ready to go anywhere and do anything, up to and including violence. This extreme right wing possessed zeal for a holy revolution in which the pagans as well as renegade and borderline Jews would be definitively defeated. Thus, the word zeal in connection with Saul's extreme zeal for the traditions of his fathers, his faultless observance of the law, and persecution of the church marks him therefore as a Shammaite Pharisee—and one of the strictest of the strict.

Convinced that God's kingdom would come very soon—that the real return from exile was about to happen—Saul viewed his own vocation as being called to bring that about. Israel had been chosen to be the covenant people of the Creator God, to be the light that would enlighten the dark world, the people through whom God would undo the sin of Adam and its effects. However, Israel had fallen into sin. Although Israel had returned geographically from her exile, the real exilic condition was not yet finished: the Romans and the pseudo-king, Herod, ruled, the temple had not yet been rebuilt, the Messiah had not yet arrived.

So, Saul of Tarsus and his Shammaite colleagues were not interested in an abstract, timeless, non-historical system of salvation. They were not even interested in—as we say now—going to heaven when they died. They believed in bodily resurrection at the end of this age in which God would raise them all to share in the life of the promised renewed Israel and renewed world. This fueled their zeal.

On several occasions Paul painfully referred to his earlier persecutions of the church in his efforts to destroy it. So why did this Greek-speaking

13

Diaspora Jew, turned Pharisaic neophyte, embark on a persecution of the churches in Jerusalem and even as far as Damascus? Within a few years of Jesus' death, the Greek-speaking Jewish Christian Stephen (Acts 6:8–60) was accused of blaspheming against God, Moses, and the temple, saying that Jesus of Nazareth would destroy "this place" (i.e., the temple) and change the customs Moses handed down to the Jews. Thus, the charge against Stephen involved Jesus' own criticism of the temple and the promoting of Jesus' own approach to the Torah. A Judean mob might well regard this as an affront to their own convictions and aspirations: a charge, in other words, of disloyalty to Israel's ancestral customs, a disloyalty that might be disastrous. For this he was stoned to death by an unruly mob—with Saul's presence and consent. However, Stephen was not put to death on account of anything that could be called heresy over some complicated theological issue, but more out of sectarian rivalry, for promoting Jesus' revolutionary vision of Israel in which the temple would be judged and elements of the Torah set aside in the light of the dawning of the kingdom of God.

In addition, James, the brother of John, was put to death by Herod Agrippa around 41–44 A.D., which met with Jewish approval (Acts 12:1–2). Approximately the year 62 A.D., the high priest Annas had James, the "brother" of Jesus and some of his friends, stoned to death on the charge of being breakers of the law. Yet, it is highly unlikely that James was an actual lawbreaker, since there is no indication that members of the Jerusalem church had abandoned the Torah. To the contrary, they seem to have been strictly observant, especially the circle associated with James. It may be that James and his colleagues were put to death for simply being different, socio-religious deviants who combined veneration of Jesus within a thoroughly Jewish way of life.

Also, the letter of James is strongly outspoken in its condemnation of the wealthy aristocracy, which would have made for powerful enemies. In addition, James might also have borne the brunt of Jewish opposition to Paul and his coworkers, who in their activity in the wider world—from Jerusalem's point of view—were brazenly fraternizing with gentiles and allegedly discouraging Diaspora Jews from observing the Torah. This was precisely what the members of the delegation from James to Antioch were afraid would happen, which is why they asked Jewish Christians to separate from gentiles in Antioch (Gal 2). Paul's sharp opposition to this request must have been seen as highly dangerous back in Jerusalem, and, in a sense, James' own death later proved the point.

Thus, the Pharisees, whose hope for the kingdom of God were marked by ever stricter observance of the Torah, as well as a passionate attachment to the temple, were bound to see the early Jesus followers as dangerously disloyal. If that sort of belief were to catch on, it could delay or even derail the long-awaited fulfillment of the divine purposes. Also, Jews would have considered blasphemous the veneration of a crucified man as Messiah and Lord, especially if, as seems likely, worship ascribed to YHWH was being given to Jesus. For this reason Saul of Tarsus persecuted the church.

Paul informed us that he persecuted the church because he was extremely zealous for the traditions of his forefathers. More than simply hotheaded enthusiasm, his zeal had a particular resonance in Jewish tradition referring to the violence that might be necessary to preserve Israel's holiness. Several themes cluster around zeal: holiness, purity, separation, hatred of paganism, and violence. Given this background, it is not difficult to imagine a young Jew—faced with the sordid sort of paganism in the early first century and the shabby compromises of many of his countrymen—being fired up by this vision. To be a Pharisee meant to cling to God's faithfulness, to inflame one's courage, and to act.

The young Saul from Tarsus understood the word Judaism to mean the active propagation of the ancestral way of life, and its defense against attack, whether from the outside or the inside. Thus, as a faithful young Pharisee committed to Judaism, Saul believed that it was his duty to stop by whatever means necessary those who perverted Israel's worship and affronted her holiness. This was what drove Saul and his persecution of Christian Jews and non-Jews, as well as Jews he considered lax.

Given Paul's intelligence and oratorical skills, he certainly could have become a distinguished rabbi among the Pharisees, perhaps even later elevated to the ranks of the Sanhedrin. He could also have become a Pharisaic missionary to non-Jews, such as Eliezer was to a royal family. Like Philo, he could have been a leading figure in the protests against Caligula's attempts to install a statue of himself in the Jerusalem temple in the year 40 A.D. Like his younger contemporary Josephus, he also might have played a significant part in the Judean revolt against Rome in 66 A.D. We can only guess at why he did not do this. However, what we do know is that something dramatic and radical happened to Saul of Tarsus in the midst of his persecution of the church. As a result, people would soon be saying of him: "The man who formerly persecuted us is now preaching the faith he once tried to destroy" (Gal 1:23). What transformed Saul the zealous Pharisee into St. Paul, Christianity's premier apostolic mystic, who, apart from Jesus, was more formative for re-organizing the Jewish worldview around messianic hopes and establishing kingdom-centered Christian communities in the West?

The Transforming Event

"Saul, Saul, why do you persecute me?" (Acts 9:4)

The violent Shammaite Pharisee Saul of Tarsus' stunning transformation into Paul the first Christian apostolic mystic is related in Acts of the Apostles 9:1–9:

> Meanwhile, Saul was still breathing out murderous threats against the Lord's disciples. He went to the high priest and asked him for letters to the synagogues in Damascus, so that if he found any there who belonged to the Way, whether men or women, he might take them as prisoners to Jerusalem. As he neared Damascus on his journey, suddenly a light from heaven flashed around him. He fell to the ground and heard a voice say to him, "Saul, Saul, why do you persecute me?" "Who are you, Lord?" Saul asked. "I am Jesus, whom you are persecuting," he replied. "Now get up and go into the city, and you will be told what you must do." The men traveling with Saul stood there speechless; they heard the sound but did not see anyone.

In repeating this story three times (Acts 9; 22; 26), Luke wanted to link Paul with the prophets and visionaries of Israel's history. He also wished to place him alongside penitent pagans who embraced a new way of life. Luke's three versions of the Damascus road event serve as both an apology for Paul's new life and work and an official approval of him in the eyes of potentially puzzled or hostile readers. One should call to mind that, unlike the other apostles, Paul had not lived with Jesus for three years. Luke's three versions of the Damascus-road episode also heighten the dramatic tension as the story is repeated in a crescendo to accompany Paul's progress, through riots and trials, until his final arrival in Rome.

In referring to this foundational Damascus-road event, Paul insisted that he had really seen Jesus. In 1 Corinthians 15, he wrote: "After the risen Jesus had appeared to Cephas, the Twelve, more than 500 of the brothers and sisters at one time, then to James, then to all the apostles, last of all he also appeared to me, as to one abnormally born." (The Greek for "abnormally born" is better translated as "abortion," "ripped from my mother's womb.") In his disputes with the Corinthians, Paul asked: "Have I not seen the Lord?" (1 Cor 9:1). This emphasizes the unexpected and traumatic happening of meeting the person Jesus-Messiah, whose followers Paul had been trying to kill.

The first chapter of Ezekiel became an important text for devout Jews of Saul's time and later. N. T. Wright[2] suggests that Paul was meditating on this text while traveling to Damascus. In one of the strangest scenes in all scripture, the prophet sees the heavenly throne-chariot upon which the One is seated, the whirling and flashing wheels, the strange four-faced creatures that inhabit them, and then something that seemed like a human form. As a consequence, the prophet falls on his face as though dead. A throne vision would be about heaven and earth coming together. It would have to do with the long-awaited renewal of creation itself—the ultimate prophetic vision. However, on the Damascus road Saul came face-to-face with Jesus of Nazareth.

This fulfillment of Israel's ancient scriptures utterly contradicted the way Paul had been reading them until then. In raising Jesus-Messiah bodily from the dead, God proclaimed not only that he really was Israel's Messiah, but also that this Jesus had done what the one true God promised to do himself, in person. And Jesus was addressing Saul as a master addresses a slave. Saul-Paul was later to proclaim that heaven and earth come together in Jesus-Messiah and the apostle reoriented his entire life around this fact accordingly. However, Saul never stopped believing in the one God of Abraham, Isaac, and Jacob. Years later he would write of glimpsing the glory of God in the face of Jesus-Messiah. The Damascus event was all about Jesus. Exactly as the martyr Stephen had claimed, heaven and earth were now held together, fused together. This underscored Jesus-Messiah as being in person the reality toward which the temple itself had pointed and he believed that the one God had acted decisively and conclusively in, and even as, Israel's Messiah.

Thus, Paul made the astonishing claim that he had seen the risen Christ even after the ascension. He did not use the language of interior spiritual or religious experiences but the language that described the encounter with a really living but transformed person. Jew and non-Jew alike in Paul's day understood resurrection only in terms of bodily resurrection. A non-bodily resurrection would have been considered an

---

2. Wright, *Paul: Biography*, 50–57.

oxymoron. As mentioned in Romans 1, Paul understood Jesus as being marked out as the Son of God, that is the Messiah, by the Spirit of holiness through his bodily resurrection, which established Jesus as the true Messiah, the true bearer of Israel's God-engendered destiny. Paul's encounter with the risen Christ and jolting awareness of Jesus as having been raised bodily from the dead are of paramount importance for understanding his life-changing experience on the Damascus road.

This earth-shattering mystical incident cannot and should be spiritualized or psychologized. Saul-Paul (Paul means "small" in Greek) had become a new man, the first Jewish Christian apostolic mystic who would write: "It is no longer I who live, but it is Christ who lives in me" (Gal 2:20). This violent opponent of Jesus' followers now had a new heart and declared: "The love of Christ urges us on" (2 Cor 5:14). He could write about his Shammaite mind-change: "For who has known the mind of the Lord so as to instruct him? But we have the mind of Christ" (1 Cor 2:16) as well as "we destroy arguments and every proud obstacle raised up against the knowledge of God, and we take every thought captive to obey Christ" (2 Cor 10:5). In short, Paul now had a Christ-drenched worldview and a Christ-inundated heart that would prompt him to proclaim: "For God, who said, 'Let light shine out of darkness,' made his light shine in our hearts to give us the light of the knowledge of God's glory displayed in the face of Christ" (2 Cor 4:6). In this light, Paul would not only rethink his entire Jewish tradition—which he never abandoned—but he also came to understand the Jewish scriptures in the light of the crucified and risen Messiah and his Holy Spirit.

We read further in Acts of the Apostle:

> Saul got up from the ground, but when he opened his eyes he could see nothing. So they led him by the hand into Damascus. For three days he was blind, and did not eat or drink anything. In Damascus there was a disciple named Ananias. The Lord called to him in a vision, "Ananias!" "Yes, Lord," he answered. The Lord told him, "Go to the house of Judas on Straight Street and ask for a man from Tarsus named Saul, for he is praying. In a vision he has seen a man named Ananias come and place his hands on him to restore his sight." "Lord," Ananias answered, "I have heard many reports about this man and all the harm he has done to your holy people in Jerusalem. And he has come here with authority from the chief priests to arrest all who call on your name." But the Lord said to Ananias, "Go! This man is my chosen instrument to proclaim my

name to the Gentiles, their kings, and to the people of Israel. I will show him how much he must suffer for my name." Then Ananias went to the house and entered it. Placing his hands on Saul, he said, "brother Saul, the Lord Jesus, who appeared to you on the road as you were coming here—has sent me so that you may see again and be filled with the Holy Spirit." Immediately, something like scales fell from Saul's eyes, and he could see again. He got up and was baptized. (Acts 9:8–18)

Three things that Jesus had told Ananias about Saul should be noted. First, that Paul was praying—seemingly the *Shema*, "Hear, O Israel, the LORD is our God, the LORD is one." Second, Jesus chose Saul to be the one through whom Jesus' good news would go out to the world. Third, Saul would have to suffer much for Jesus' sake. That Ananias addressed Saul as "brother" seems incongruous. Of course, at this point all Jesus' followers were Jews, so there was already a sense of extended kinship within which this new reality had arisen. However, Paul would later write that there is "no longer Greek nor Jew, slave or free, male or female, you are all one in Christ Jesus" (Gal 3:28)—in part, meaning that the degrees of nearness to God had been eliminated. This truth was already contained within Ananias' opening greeting, "brother Saul."

Then, something like scales fell from Saul's eyes. Jesus' early followers knew very well that, just as Jesus himself had gone about healing people, so they too were entrusted with this gift.

Then Ananias baptized the puzzled Saul, which happened as soon as a person came to believe in the crucified Jesus as the risen Lord. Jesus-Messiah had used the language of baptism to speak of his approaching death. To be baptized was therefore to die and rise with Jesus-Messiah.

Because baptism was like branding a slave, the branded slave Saul-Paul now belonged to the Messiah and received Jesus' own Holy Spirit. Like a medieval town crier walking through the streets with a bell, he went immediately to the Damascus synagogue to proclaim publicly that the Son of God, a new King, Jesus-Messiah, had been placed on the throne. This was certainly how the word *gospel*—which originally meant the announcement of a new emperor or his arrival in a city—would be heard right across the Roman world of that day. Israel's hope had been fulfilled! The King has been enthroned! Paul was declaring that the crucified Jesus was Israel's long-awaited Messiah. *Jesus* is Lord, not Caesar.

Paul went even further in his later writings when he daringly applied to Jesus what God had proclaimed in Isaiah 45:22–23: "For I am God, and there is no other. . . . Before me every knee will bend; by me every tongue will swear." In his Epistle to the Philippians 2:9-11, Paul wrote: "Therefore God exalted him to the highest place and gave him the name that is above every name, that at the name of Jesus every knee should bend, in heaven and on earth and under the earth, and every tongue acknowledge that Jesus Christ is Lord, to the glory of God the Father." Thus, if Jesus were exalted to share the very throne of God, to share the very glory that God would not share with another, then this Jesus must have been from all eternity, somehow or other, equal with God. Messianic views were varied in this period. Some Jews show no evidence of having any interest in a messiah (Sirach). Others write of a royal messiah (Psalms of Solomon) and others of a priestly messiah (Qumran). Others focused on a transcendent messiah (1 Enoch). Some, however, expected a warrior-messiah, a new David who would overthrow the evil pagans and restore the temple so that God's glory—which left the temple during the Babylonian sacking of Jerusalem—would at last return. Then, a worldwide rule of justice and peace would be established.

I have purposely avoided the word *conversion* to denote Saul's Damascus-road encounter with the risen Christ. It is anachronistic to maintain that Saul converted from something we might call Judaism to something we might call Christianity. Paul definitely would not have explained what happened to him that way. (Jesus' followers were called Christians for the first time in Antioch, around the year 30 C.E. [Acts 11:26].) Martin Luther and many others experienced conversion in the sense of a newly felt knowledge of God's grace and personal love that sharply contrasted with all they previously knew. Faith, grace, and scripture alone became their cry.

However, this meaning of conversion also cannot be predicated of Saul of Tarsus. He was not trying to earn his own salvation by hard moral effort and needing it to learn about previously unknown qualities called grace and faith—as opposed to works. This implies a deep misunderstanding and devaluation of Second Temple Judaism and of Pharisaism in particular. Moreover, in Paul's view, one was a follower of Jesus-Messiah *within* a thoroughly Jewish frame of reference. He did not reject everything about his Jewish way of life. Nor for that matter did he keep them all and merely place Jesus-Messiah on the top. For him, the crucified and risen Jesus-Messiah perfected his Judaism—brought it to its long awaited goal. Neither Jesus nor Paul founded another religion. Jesus and others repeatedly gave Jews priority in their mission and stressed that he came for Israel's sake, not that of the gentiles. Did not Jesus proclaim: "salvation is from the Jews" (John 4:22).

Christians are a community of eschatologically renewed Jews and pilgrim nations united in the Messiah as an expanded end-time Israel, which recent popes have called "spiritual Jews." Christianity is not another religion but Judaism completed—a view Paul definitively held.

However, a tension does exist in the New Testament. On the one hand, we read in Luke 22:20: "In the same way, after the supper [Jesus] took the cup, saying, 'This cup is the new covenant in my blood, which is poured out for you.'" The author of the Letter to the Hebrews appeals to Jeremiah 31:31, who prophesied: "The days are coming," declares the LORD, "when I will make a new covenant with the people of Israel and with the people of Judah," when he wrote: "By calling this covenant 'new,' he has made the first one obsolete; and what is obsolete and outdated will soon disappear" (Heb 8:13). On the other hand, in Romans 9: 2–5 Paul wrote this about the people of Israel: "Theirs is the adoption to sonship; theirs the divine glory, the covenants, the receiving of the law, the temple worship and the promises. Theirs are the patriarchs, and from them is traced the human ancestry of the Messiah, who is God over all, forever praised!" and in Romans 11: 1–2 asked: "Then: Did God reject his people? By no means! I am an Israelite myself, a descendant of Abraham, from the tribe of Benjamin. God did not reject his people, whom he foreknew."[3] He also emphasized: "first to the Jew, then to the gentile" (Rom 1:16).

Thus, I do not share the position called supersessionism that because Paul worshipped the crucified and risen Jesus-Messiah as Lord, the Mosaic covenant is null and void. Neither do I agree with those scholars who hold a dual-covenant theology, an "inferiorsessionism" (my term), which holds that the Mosaic covenant remains, *without qualifications*, valid for Jews. Did not Jesus say in Matthew's Gospel: "Do not think that I have come to abolish the Law or the Prophets; I have not come to abolish them but to *fulfill* them" (Matt 5:17, my emphasis)? Did not Jesus shed tears because his own refused to accept his way of being Jewish? Did not the rejection of Jesus by his own produce a crisis in Paul's life? Paul lamented: "I have great sorrow and unceasing anguish in my heart. For I could wish that I myself were cursed and cut off from Christ for the sake of my people, those of my own race, the people of Israel" (Rom 9:2–4). What is one to make of these words of Paul: "But if their *transgression* means riches for the world, and their loss means riches for the Gentiles, how much greater riches will their

---

3. For a brilliant exegesis of the highly disputed chapters, Romans 9–11, see Wright, *Paul and the Faithfulness of God*, 1156–1258.

full inclusion bring! I am talking to you Gentiles. Inasmuch as I am the apostle to the Gentiles, I take pride in my ministry in the hope that I may somehow arouse my own people to envy and save some of them. For if their *rejection* brought reconciliation to the world, what will their *acceptance* be but life from the dead?" (Rom 11: 12–15, my emphasis).

My own view depends upon the theology of sublation,[4] that is, what sublates (the new covenant because of the divine Jesus-Messiah's death and resurrection) goes beyond what is sublated (the unrevoked Mosaic covenant), introduces something new and distinct, and puts everything on a new basis. However, so far from interfering with what is sublated or destroying it (the Jews remain God's covenanted people) the new covenant, on the contrary, needs it, includes it, and preserves all its proper features and properties, and carries them forward to a fuller realization within a richer context, that is, Christianity.

I maintain that both God's unrevoked covenant to the Jews and the new covenant prophesied by Jeremiah 31:31 were embedded in Jesus' and Paul's very *being* and they both lived by them. They are living exemplars of what is meant by sublation. Did not the prophet Zechariah proclaim: "This is what the LORD Almighty says: 'In those days ten people from all languages and nations will take firm hold of one Jew by the hem of his robe and say, "Let us go with you, because we have heard that God is with you"'" (Zech 8:23)? Besides, the Christian Bible consists of both the Jewish scriptures and the New Testament. Vatican II's dogmatic constitution on divine revelation, *Dei verbum*, clearly teaches that,

> God, the inspirer and author of both Testaments, wisely arranged that the New Testament be hidden in the Old and the Old be made manifest in the New. For, though Christ established the new covenant in His blood (see Luke 22:20; 1 Cor. 11:25), still the books of the Old Testament with all their parts, caught up into the proclamation of the Gospel, acquire and show forth their full meaning in the New Testament (see Matt. 5:17; Luke 24:27; Rom. 16:25–26; 2 Cor. 14:16) and in turn shed light on it and explain it. (Chap. IV, no. 15)

Jesus-Messiah demonstrated this principle when he chided the Emmaus disciples and said: "'How foolish you are, and how slow to believe all that the prophets have spoken! Did not the Messiah have to suffer these things and then enter his glory?' And beginning with Moses and all the

4. Lonergan, *Method*, 241.

Prophets, he explained to them what was said in all the scriptures concerning himself" (Luke 24: 25–27).

Paul's powerful statement in his Letter to the Romans proclaimed: "Did God reject his people? By no means!" (Rom 11:1) and "I could wish that I myself were cursed and cut off from Christ for the sake of my people, those of my own race, the people of Israel. Theirs is the adoption to sonship; theirs the divine glory, the covenants, the receiving of the law, the temple worship and the promises" (Rom 9:3-4). However, the Epistle to the Hebrews states: "But in fact the ministry Jesus has received is as superior to theirs as the covenant of which he is mediator is superior to the old one, since the new covenant is established on better promises. For if there had been nothing wrong with that first covenant, no place would have been sought for another" (Heb 8:6–7). Jesus proclaimed himself as *the* way (John 14:6) and Acts of the Apostles 14:12 affirms that salvation "is found in no one else, for there is no other name [than Jesus-Messiah] under heaven given to mankind by which we must be saved." Thus, a tension does exist, but I agree with those scholars who contend that Paul saw his faith in Jesus-Messiah as precisely the fulfillment of his Judaism. Did he not write, "For Christ is the end of the law, that everyone who has faith may be justified" (Rom 10:4 NRSV).[5] In line with the Second Vatican Council document, *Nostra aetate* no. 4, I also affirm that "the Church awaits that day, known to God alone, on which all peoples will address the Lord in a single voice and 'serve him shoulder to shoulder'" (Zeph 3:9).[6]

In addition, contrary to popular belief, there was nothing in the first century corresponding to what we now call Judaism. Judaism meant simply the fervent observance of the Jewish way of life. One finds then—not Judaism in the contemporary sense—but only the many communities of Jews around the world, praying to Israel's God, studying the scriptures, and focusing on temple and the Torah. For example, although the Qumran communities were observant Jews, they were not what contemporary parlance would call Judaism. Christianity—in the contemporary sense—did not exist either. In the first century we find only groups of people who believed that the crucified and risen Jesus of Nazareth was Israel's Messiah and the world's rightful Lord—and tried to live accordingly.

5. Some translators use the word "end," or "culmination," or "goal."

6. For more on this delicate topic, see the December 2005 report from the Commission for Religious Relations with the Jews, "The Gifts and the Calling of God are Irrevocable: A Reflection on Theological Questions Pertaining to Catholic-Jewish relations on the Occasion of the 50th Anniversary of *Nostra aetate* (no. 4)."

Saul's Damascus-road experience convinced him that Israel's God had done what he always said he would do. Israel's scriptures had been fulfilled in ways never before imagined. Temple and Torah themselves were not after all the ultimate realities, but instead glorious signposts pointing forward to the new heaven and earth reality that had come to birth in the crucified and risen Jesus. Paul remained to his dying day fiercely loyal to Israel's God, seen in Jesus' light and inspired by Jesus' Holy Spirit. Paul and his communities focused on the belief that the one God had acted climatically and decisively in, and even as, Israel's Messiah.

Saul-Paul came to the realization that the one true God had done for Jesus of Nazareth, in the middle of time, what Saul-Paul thought God was going to do for Israel at the end of time. God had vindicated Jesus after his sufferings at the hands of the pagans. The resurrection demonstrated to Saul-Paul that Jesus' followers were right and that he—who had considered Jesus an anti-messiah—was wrong. What he wrote in Romans 1 offers an excellent summary of his world view and the true gospel:

> Paul, a servant of Christ Jesus, called to be an apostle and set apart for the gospel of God—the gospel he promised beforehand through his prophets in the Holy Scriptures regarding his Son, who as to his earthly life was a descendant of David, and who through the Spirit of holiness was appointed the Son of God in power by his resurrection from the dead: Jesus Christ our Lord. Through him we received grace and apostleship to call all the Gentiles to the obedience that comes from faith for his name's sake. And you also are among those Gentiles who are called to belong to Jesus Christ.

From Paul's perspective, if Jesus really were the Messiah and if his death and resurrection really were the decisive God-sent defeat of sin and the vindication of God's people, then this meant that the age to come had already begun—what God had been planning all along occurred in the apocalyptic fulfillment of the covenant through the crucified and risen Jesus-Messiah. Thus, the present age and the promised age to come overlapped.

In Romans 1:16 Paul strangely wrote: "I am not ashamed of the gospel." Why be ashamed? Deuteronomy 21 teaches that he who hangs upon a tree is cursed. Even more startling, Paul wrote in 2 Corinthians 5:21: "God made him who had no sin to be sin for us." Thus, a cursed, crucified Messiah who had been made sin made no sense either to Jews or gentiles. The ridicule heaped upon those who preached such a gospel must have been enormous. Yet Paul defended his gospel: "Jews demand signs and Greeks look for wisdom, but we preach Christ crucified: a stumbling block to

Jews and foolishness to Gentiles. But to those whom God has called, both Jews and Greeks, Christ the power of God and the wisdom of God" (1 Cor 1:22–24). The Damascus encounter was a call, in the sense of a vocation, from the one God whom Paul continued to worship. This calling commissioned him to proclaim to the non-Jewish peoples the crucified and risen one, Jesus-Messiah, as God's power and wisdom.

Thus, I emphasize the *continuity* between the Jewish Shammaite Pharisee Saul of Tarsus and Paul the apostle: the same God, the same religion, the same overall narratives. The Damascus-road episode, while not the only thing that shaped his epistles, was nonetheless the catalyst for and the lens through which he viewed YHWH, Jesus, messiahship, Holy Spirit, Israel, Torah, justification, gentiles, and hope.

Paul's letter to the Galatians 1:15 well summarizes Paul's new vocation: "But when God, who set me apart from my mother's womb and called me by his grace, was pleased to reveal his Son in me so that I might preach him among the Gentiles, my immediate response was not to consult any human being." This was the most important aspect of Paul's transformation: his new evaluation of Jesus-Messiah and the only time Paul refers explicitly to what happened to him—or better yet in him—on the Damascus road. There is nothing about repentance and faith; nothing about finding his heart strangely warmed; nothing about replacing works with faith. This is a call, like that of the ancient prophets.

In addition, when Paul wrote of Jesus as appearing to him, the result was the particular commission he received and the particular task he was given—"set me apart from my mother womb and called me by his grace." Grace was the fresh divine power at work not so much upon him as through him. Paul wrote elsewhere of the divine grace not simply in connection with justification or salvation but especially in connection with the apostolic vocation. For example, in Galatians 2:9 Paul emphasized, somewhat sarcastically: "James, Cephas, and John, those esteemed as pillars, gave me and Barnabas the right hand of fellowship when they recognized *the grace given to me*. They agreed that we should go to the Gentiles, and they to the circumcised" (my emphasis). And in Romans 15:15–20, Paul again linked *grace* with his *priestly* ministry of proclaiming the gospel:

> Yet I have written to you quite boldly on some points to remind you of them again, because of the *grace* God gave me to be a minister of Christ Jesus to the Gentiles. He gave me the *priestly* duty of proclaiming the gospel of God, so that the Gentiles might become

an offering acceptable to God, sanctified by the Holy Spirit. Therefore I glory in Christ Jesus in my service to God. (My emphasis)

The Damascus event prompted Paul to describe and anchor God's
radically new deed in Jesus-Messiah to Israel's ancient traditions to which,
he contended, he was still absolutely loyal. Paul now regarded himself as a
prophetic figure, heralding the gospel of God's new exodus, and the arrival
of the true Davidic deliverer among Jews and gentiles across the eastern
Mediterranean. The monumental alteration focused on Jesus-Messiah himself. Israel's God revealed his Son not only to Saul but also *in* Saul. What Paul
wrote in Galatians 2:20 gets right to the heart of Paul's identity: "I live, not I,
but Jesus lives in me." This explains what YHWH wanted to do through Paul,
namely, to broadcast the good news to the nations. What happened to Paul
was his call and commission to be an apostle, or rather the apostle to the
nations. Persecuting the church stopped and announcing the crucified and
risen Jesus-Messiah, God's very own Son, to the nations began.

Thus, what mattered for Paul was not that he had had a particular
kind of experience but that he had encountered Israel's Messiah and now
knew that Israel's Messiah had been crucified and raised bodily from the
dead. Paul was the kind of teacher who wanted people to work out, to think
through, and then to live out what had in fact happened to Jesus-Messiah
and therefore what had happen to them through baptism into the Messiah.
In Romans 6:10–11 we read: "The death [Jesus-Messiah] died, he died to
sin once for all; but the life he lives, he lives to God. In the same way, count
yourselves dead to sin but alive to God in [Jesus-Messiah]." Paul insisted
on the nonnegotiable transformation that consisted of the cross itself, not
as a private spiritual experience, but as a public messianic event to which
one was joined in baptism. One was thereby bound to the Messiah's cross,
the Messiah's faithfulness, the Messiah's life, and the Messiah's love. Thus,
for Paul, the divine call on the road to Damascus meant being grasped by
and incorporated into all Israel's redeeming realities. Saul became Paul, the
Christianity's premier apostolic mystic.

Paul's Mystical-Prophetic Confirmation in Arabia

"I went into Arabia." (Gal 1:17)

Paul's Letter to the Galatians offers enticing insights into the reasons for
his apostolic convictions. From the very beginning of the letter he claimed

that his apostleship derived not from any human source but from Jesus-Messiah and God the Father who raised Christ from the dead. This commissioned him to announce the good news about Jesus-Messiah among the nations. Therefore, he admonished the Galatians for "so quickly deserting the one who called you to live in the grace of Christ and . . . turning to a different gospel—which is really no gospel at all" (Gal 1:6–7). He reminded them again that the gospel he preached is not of human origin (Gal 1:11) and that if anyone is preaching to them a different gospel, then "let them be under God's curse" (Gal 1:9).

This intriguing statement points out that he did not immediately discuss the Damascus event with flesh and blood nor check it out with the Jerusalem apostles (Gal 1:17). Three years passed before Paul went to Jerusalem for two weeks, speaking only with Cephas-Peter and the apostle James. As Joseph Fitzmyer said in class: "You can be certain that they did not spend their time talking about the Boston Red Sox but about the gospel of Jesus-Messiah."

Fourteen years later Paul went up to Jerusalem again because of a revelation. There he explained privately to "those esteemed as leaders" (Gal 2:2) the gospel that he was proclaiming among the gentiles to ensure that he was correct. Thus, even Paul sought official church sanction for his mission. Later, because those whom Paul called pseudo-family members from Jerusalem had been secretly smuggled into Jesus-Messiah communities to convince them that male gentile converts must be circumcised, Paul heatedly wrote: "We did not give in to them for a moment, so that the truth of the gospel might be preserved for you" (Gal 2:5). He had already challenged this "really no gospel at all" (Gal 1:7) when he alerted them to the fact that "not even Titus, who was with me, was compelled to be circumcised, even though he was a Greek" (Gal 2:3).

Especially unsettling for Paul was that Cephas-Peter, who had been eating with gentiles, drew back and separated himself from the gentiles because he was afraid of the circumcision troublemakers. The rest of the Jews—even Barnabas—did the same, joining him in this charade. So, when Cephas-Peter came to Antioch, Paul confronted him face-to-face and told him he was dead wrong for compromising the gospel truth. In front of everyone, he rebuked Cephas: "You are a Jew, yet you live like a Gentile and not like a Jew. How is it, then, that you force Gentiles to follow Jewish customs?" (Gal 2:14). In addition, Paul's epistle fiercely denounced the Galatians as "witless" and "bewitched" for believing the proponents who insisted that the male gentile believers must be circumcised. The advocates of this bogus gospel were accursed and Paul thundered: "circumcision? I wish that those agitators would go the whole way and castrate themselves!" (Gal 5:12).

Therefore, Paul's letters reveal him as a passionate and uncompromising apostle of the gospel—one who would use strong language and assert his apostolic authority. Another example: in his disagreements with the Corinthian communities, he stressed: "Am I not an apostle? Have I not seen Jesus our Lord? Are you not the result of my work in the Lord?" (1 Cor 9:1). He contemptuously claimed that so-called "super-apostles" (2 Cor 11:5) were preaching a different gospel and a skewed Jesus different from the one he proclaimed. They are *false* apostles, not super apostles, who masqueraded as apostles of Jesus-Messiah (2 Cor 11:13). He threw down the gauntlet and wrote: "I ought to have been commended by you, for I am not in the least inferior to the 'super-apostles,' even though I am nothing" (2 Cor 12:11).

Still, Paul went on to humble himself by confessing: "For I am the least of the apostles and do not even deserve to be called an apostle, because I persecuted the church of God" (1 Cor 15:9). Paul's Epistle to the Galatians repeats his gravest sin, the one he most regretted: "For you have heard of my previous way of life in Judaism, how intensely I persecuted the church of God and tried to destroy it" (Gal 1:13). In his Letter to the Ephesians (Eph 3:8), he lamented: "I am the very least of all the saints" and in 1 Timothy 1:13 he confessed: "Even though I was once a blasphemer and a persecutor and a violent man, I was shown mercy because I acted in ignorance and unbelief." The self-proclaimed "super-apostles" of Corinth did not have that kind of humility and transparency.

The Galatian letter also cryptically relates that Paul went into Arabia and then later back to Damascus. So why Arabia? Some scholars maintain that the Damascus-road episode so disrupted Saul's life that he needed a vacation and to get away from it all. Others speculate that he went into Arabia to get to proclaim his newly found gospel concerning Jesus-Messiah. However, those scholars who argue that Saul went into Arabia to have his Damascus-road calling further confirmed and deepened have the better arguments.

I have already mentioned that the young Saul of Tarsus was, in the technical Jewish sense, extremely *zealous* for his ancestral traditions. The prophet Elijah, who had tricked and killed the worshipers of the fertility god Baal, was one of Saul's heroes who catalyzed his journey into Arabia.

Elijah's victory angered queen Jezebel, a Baal worshipper, and Elijah ran for his life to Mount Sinai/Horeb in Arabia. Complaining to God that he was the last loyalist, a powerful revelation of wind, earthquake, and fire, followed by a small still voice, took place. God commanded Elijah to return to Damascus in order to anoint another prophet, Elisha, to replace him and also to anoint new kings for Syria and Israel. In addition, God declared to the bewildered prophet that he would leave 7,000 in Israel—the faithful remnant—who would remain loyal. In Romans 11:3, Paul likened himself to Elijah as the focal point of a faithful remnant and declared, "Lord, they have killed your prophets and torn down your altars; I am the only one left, and they are trying to kill me."

The word Arabia in this context refers to Mount Sinai/Horeb area. Mount Sinai, of course, was the location of the burning bush where God had given Moses the Ten Commandments. This place of revelation, of the Torah, is where the covenant between God and Israel—established earlier with Abraham, Isaac, and Jacob—was solemnly ratified. Mount Sinai/Horeb, the great mountain in Arabia, was in that sense the place of beginnings. Mount Sinai/Horeb was where Elijah had gone when his life went awry.

Thus, Saul, like Elijah, made a pilgrimage to Sinai/Horeb in order to go back to the place where the covenant was confirmed. He wanted to present himself before the one God to explain that he, too, had been extremely zealous, but that on the Damascus road his entire worldview had been shattered. There he received his instructions: go back and proclaim the new King, the crucified and risen Jesus. The Arabia journey reveals something about Paul's own self-awareness and perhaps even a touch of his confusion about his zeal as a persecutor of Jesus-followers and now as one zealous for the gospel of Jesus-Messiah. Mount Sinai/Horeb helped him to deepen his conviction that the one who took him by surprise on the Damascus Road really was Israel's fulfillment. The surprising but ultimately satisfying goal of the ancient purposes delineated by the God-given Mosaic law on Mount Sinai/Horeb had been attained in Jesus-Messiah.

Thus, Paul's loyalty to the one God of Israel was as firm as ever. Paul was never a traitor to the Jewish world. (And the claim of some scholars that Paul had never really understood the Jewish world in the first place is as absurd as it is incorrect.) Because YHWH's plan came to fruition in Jesus crucified and risen, this meant that a whole new stage of the previously barely suspected divine purpose had been initiated. It also signified that the Torah itself must be seen in an entirely new light. And Saul, like Elijah, was told to go back and begin his new mission. A few new kings and also a prophet were to be anointed by Elijah. Saul of Tarsus was to return and commence his prophetic task of announcing that Jesus of Nazareth was the true anointed king, the Messiah, the world's rightful sovereign—the Lord.

When Paul wrote in the first chapter of his Letter to the Galatians that God had set him apart from his mother's womb, he was deliberately echoing the call of the prophet Jeremiah. When he wrote of God unveiling his Son *in* him—again, *in* him not *to* him—he was using the language of Jewish mystics and seers who spoke of that unveiling or revelation as constituting a divine commissioning. When Paul wrote that the Jerusalem church later glorified God because of him, he was echoing the prophet Isaiah who wrote in chapter 49:3: "God said to me, you are my servant, Israel, in whom I will display my splendor."

In the second chapter of Galatians, Paul both wondered whether he might be running or might have run in vain and yet asserted for himself the prophetic role of God's servant. This resonates with Isaiah 49:4–6:

> But I said, "I have labored in vain; I have spent my strength for nothing at all." . . . And now the LORD says—he who formed me in the womb to be his servant to bring Jacob back to him and gather Israel to himself, for I am honored in the eyes of the LORD and my God has been my strength—he says: "It is too small a thing for you to be my servant to restore the tribes of Jacob and bring back those of Israel I have kept. I will also make you a light for the Gentiles, that my salvation may reach to the ends of the earth."

Thus, Paul, the apostolic mystic-prophet, went back to Damascus, certain that his vocation and commissioning had placed him in the ancient prophetic tradition, whether of Isaiah, Jeremiah, or Elijah himself. As a mystic-prophet he would proclaim God's truth and his anointed king, Jesus crucified and risen, to Israel and the nations.

Because of Paul's appeal to the prophets of biblical Judaism, it should be emphasized that these extraordinary people, sometimes schools of them, entered the stage of Israel's history like a strange, elemental, explosive force. Contrary to common views, the biblical prophets were not fore-tellers but *forth*-tellers who spoke God's word, not their own. I know of no other religion—except Christianity, whose roots are Jewish—that has prophets in the biblical sense. The prophetic phrase, "thus says the LORD," highlights the special intimacy the Jews enjoyed with a God who actually spoke to them. Their strong awareness of God's presence sensitized them to what was happening in Israel socially, politically, economically, militarily, and morally. Deeply aware of Israel's past, their message was often framed this way: when you so acted in the past, God did this. You are doing this now, therefore God will so act in the future. The prophetic emphasis was on the present and only then on the future in light of the past.

Referred to as the conscience of Israel, the prophets stressed that the prerequisite of political stability was social justice—that individuals were responsible for the just social structures of their society as well as for their own direct personal dealings. YHWH, who created on the basis of both mercy and justice, had high standards and would not put up with his people's exploitation, corruption, and mediocrity. The prophets found themselves in a time that was shot through with inequities, special privilege, and injustices of the most flagrant sort. Convinced that every human being, simply by virtue of his or her humanity, was a child of God and therefore in possession of rights, the prophets challenged even kings, who were merely exercising the universally accepted prerogatives of royalty. In short, the biblical prophets were apostolic mystics, as was Paul.

Thus, I do not share the erroneous view of those scholars who agree with German-born Israeli philosopher and historian Gershom Scholem[7] that it would be absurd to call Moses, the man of God, a mystic, or to apply this term to the prophets, on the strength of their immediate religious experience. This is paradigmatic of the false assumption that the experience of undifferentiated unity (atman is brahman), the fusion experience of monism, or ecstatic experiences are the hallmarks of all mysticism. Did not Abraham, Jacob, Moses, Samuel, and other patriarchs of the Jewish scriptures experience God's intimate call, have their faith tested, and wrestle with God? Were they not blessed by him? Did they not speak to him as a personal friend? Were they not often afraid and speechless in his presence, ecstatically drawn to him as a greatest good, and visibly transformed by their encounters with him? Were they not convinced that he was with his people in all they did and underwent? Did not both Moses and Jacob claim face-to-face encounters with God, even if questions remain as to how directly they gazed into his face? When Job could say to God, "but now my eyes have seen you" (Job 42:5), did not his agonizing questions cease?

The same can be said analogously of the great Jewish prophets. For example, Elijah, Isaiah, Jeremiah, Ezekiel, Hosea, and Amos were called in a most intimate way to be God's spokesmen. Often visions and ecstatic

7. Scholem, *Jewish Mysticism*, 6–7.

encounters grounded their calling. God's word burning in their hearts render them both powerless to speak it and yet incapable of holding it in. Their authorization to speak God's word often came because they had stood in "the counsel of the LORD" (Jer 23:18). This means that false prophets had no access to God's assembly and thus did not know God's secrets. What the false prophets said came not from God but from their own evil imaginations. The genuine prophets' felt-knowledge of God resulted in their invincible trust in God's faithfulness, tenderness, compassion, love, and wrath. Genuine mystical experience is profoundly transforming—resulting in a new consciousness and heart, a new person with a new way of life. These God-haunted, God-possessed, God-illuminated, and God-transformed individuals became Israel's conscience. Having received God's Spirit into their hearts, they prophesied a time when God's faithful people would definitively receive the Holy Spirit. This is mysticism and the Jewish prophets were essentially apostolic mystics—mystics in action.

Of course, Paul, the apostolic mystic, became both Israel's and Christianity's premier prophet. He came to understand Israel's past in the light of Jesus-Messiah, who brought that past to fulfillment. In Paul's view, "Christianity" was Judaism completed, perfected. He understood Israel's and the world's present and future in light of Jesus crucified and risen. It fascinates me that Christianity's premier apostolic mystic-prophet concentrated his apostolic journeys to and in Roman colonies, thus proclaiming Jesus the Lord who was replacing Caesar.

Only Paul, the premier apostolic mystic-prophet, could have written these words:

> In your relationships with one another, have the same mind as Christ Jesus: Who, being in very nature God, did not consider equality with God something to be used to his own advantage; rather, he made himself nothing by taking the very nature of a servant, being made in human likeness. And being found in appearance as a man, he humbled himself by becoming obedient to death—even death on a cross! Therefore God exalted him to the highest place and gave him the name that is above every name, that at the name of Jesus every knee should bow, in heaven and on earth and under the earth, and every tongue acknowledge that Jesus Christ is Lord, to the glory of God the Father. (Phil 2:5–11)

Chapter 2

The Apostle Paul, Christianity's Premier Apostolic Mystic

Incorrect Views of Christian Mysticism

"There are no Protestant mystics and even if there were some, there should not be any."[1]

THE HASTINGS ENCYCLOPEDIA OF RELIGIONS AND ETHICS lists well over 100 definitions of mysticism, with most of them reflecting the bias of the authors more than the realities of the Christian mystical life. For example, genuine Christian mysticism cannot be reduced to madness, hysteria, escaping the pressures of daily life, self-hypnosis, repressed eroticism, or regression to the earliest sensations of childhood—for example, nursing at the mother's breast. Because of the erotic imagery Christian mystics sometimes used to explain their experiences, Freudians judge what they wrote—sometimes in terms of the biblical Song of Songs—to be sublimated sexual experiences. The works of Julia Kristeva offer an especially good presentation of this view. Saints Augustine of Hippo and Ignatius of Loyola, to offer just two examples, had ample sexual experience before their conversions, but what they described about their later mystical lives is like comparing a popular soft drink to the finest French cognac. On a personal note, I have had contact with contemplative nuns who had been sexually active before their entry into religious life. The profound mystics among them would deny any resemblance between their former and current life.

Carl Jung and others regarded mystics as heretics who disguised their explosive experiences with orthodox language. However, no genuine

1. Walter T. Stace, cited by Fremantle, *Protestant Mystics*, vii.

Christian mystic alters the relation between mystical experiences, states, life, and church doctrine. Genuine Christian mystics deepen the tradition, and, at times, of course, cause tensions with church authorities in their attempt to describe in new ways their encounter with the ineffable. Are not bishops, cardinals, popes, and other major figures, whose mysticism and orthodoxy are beyond question, to be found in the Christian mystical tradition? The premier scholar of the Western mystical tradition, Bernard McGinn, Professor Emeritus of the University of Chicago, has definitively shown in his multi-volume works the congruence between the mystical life and orthodoxy.

Aldous Huxley and Timothy Leary—to name but two—have popularized the notion that mystical experiences can be had by ingesting psychedelic drugs.[2] However, the fairly well-known writer Peter Matthiessen offered a better insight into the effects of such drugs—but still does not get to the heart of the matter—when he wrote: "Drugs can clear away the past, enhance the present; towards the secret garden they can only point the way. Lacking the grit of discipline and insight, the drug vision remains a sort of dream that cannot be brought into daily life. Old mists may be banished, that is true, but the alien chemical agents form another mist, maintaining the separation of the 'I' from the true experience of the infinite within us."[3] Although I partially share his view, I prefer once again to emphasize *experience* in the sense that an experienced musician knows and loves music and experience—and not in the sense of discrete, transient events. Granted that Christian mystics do have mystical experiences in the popular sense, I prefer to emphasize mystical *states* and the mystical *life*. I would add that radical spiritual dereliction—better known as the dark nights of purification—and personal transformation, both witnessed in genuine Christian mysticism, far transcend what results from the "bad and good trips" of psychedelic drugs.

The eighteenth- to nineteenth-century theologian Friedrich Schleiermacher and the twentieth-century German theologian Emil Brunner sharply, but incorrectly, distinguished the *allegedly* Greek-infested Catholic mystical tradition from the word-of-God theology articulated by Martin Luther, John Calvin, St. Augustine (in his more evangelical and less Platonic moments), and supremely by the apostle Paul. In short, Catholic mysticism

2. See my criticism of such views in Egan, "Christian Mysticism and Psychedelic Drugs," 33–41.

3. Matthiessen "The Snow Leopard I," 57–58.

and God's word were understood as polar opposites. Consonant with these now largely discredited Protestant views, the late British writer, Walter T. Stace, wrote: "there are no Protestant mystics and even if there were some, there should not be any."[4] So, in Stace's opinion, Christian mysticism was a contradiction in terms. Even those commentators sympathetic to the Christian mystical tradition, Anne Fremantle, for one, held the mistaken view that all Catholic mystics—unlike their Protestant counterparts—travel a well-worn, well-known, well-marked, easily identifiable three-stage journey of purgation, illumination, and union. Both the multi-volume works of Bernard McGinn and the German scholar Kurt Ruh have shown conclusively that this is not the case.

The Reformers' hostility to Christian mysticism also originated partly from a false reading of the works of the influential fifth- or sixth-century Syrian monk Pseudo-Dionysius. However, recent scholarship has convincingly shown that he, like many before him, used Greek categories and thought but transformed them through the scriptures, the authoritative church fathers, and a biblically rich liturgical life. Not only did he judge all things in the light of Christ—the Eucharist is central to his thought—but his mysticism also remained inextricably linked to the fullness of church life with solid roots in the Greek Christian mystical tradition.

Moreover, the Protestant mistrust of things Greek overlooks that the New Testament was written in Greek, that Jesus probably and Paul undoubtedly spoke Greek, that the Greek translation of the Jewish scriptures, the Septuagint, was the Bible of many early Christians—although some continued to use the Hebrew Old Testament—and that the Reformation distinction between pure Judaism vs. Greek thought has been thoroughly discredited. The Jewish exile to and return from Babylon deeply influenced the Judaism of Jesus' and Paul's time. To this day, one can find Greek-speaking Jews in Israel.

Besides, just as the Jewish scriptures dominated Jesus' and the apostle Paul's worldview, Christian scripture permeated the mind, heart, and emotions of many mystics right up to the Reformation era and beyond. Indeed, the earliest Christian usage of the word "mystical" signified the allegorical interpretation of Scripture, especially as it disclosed Christ as the key to unlocking the secrets of the Old Testament[5]—one reason why I designate Paul as Christianity's premier apostolic mystic. Irrefutable evidence exists

4. Stace, cited by Fremantle, *The Protestant Mystics*, vii.

5. An excellent example of this can be found in Gregory of Nyssa's *Life of Moses*.

that biblical exegesis and mysticism remained inseparable throughout much of Christian history. A conviction prevailed that the very act of biblical exegesis could be mystically transformative. The perfect Christian was one who knew how to read scripture, which Paul certainly did. What is more, much Christian mysticism is rooted in biblically saturated monastic liturgical-sacramental practices. In short, those in monastic life copied, preached, sang, celebrated, enacted, and lived scripture, which opened them to that loving, direct, immediate, transformative consciousness of God: the heart of the mystical life.

Recent scholarship persuasively demonstrates that the Reformation did not introduce a definite break in the history of Christian mysticism.[6] In fact, at least in its formative first century or more, Protestantism did not lack for mystics and mystical theology. There is more continuity than break between inherited mystical traditions and what one finds in the Protestant mystics. Some scholars even argue that Luther was a mystic. Certainly, both he and Calvin made use of the themes and language found in medieval mystics. Hans Denck, Sebastian Frank, Valentin Weigel, Johann Arndt, John Donne, Henry Vaughan, Thomas Traherne, and a host of others were also Christian mystics.

In 1930, Anders Nygren, a Swedish Lutheran theologian, published his highly influential book *Eros and Agape*. He attacked Catholic mysticism for having a supposedly only *natural* striving, which he called "erotic libido." He contrasted this so-called works-Pelagian desire—that is, pulling oneself up by one's own boot straps—with agape, God's love, which takes the initiative in salvation without human yearning. However, Nygren totally missed the fact that Catholic mysticism is a charism, a special God-given calling. The anonymous author of *The Cloud of Unknowing* is paradigmatic of the view of Catholic mystics when he wrote: "without God's grace a person would be so completely insensitive to the reality of mystical prayer that he would all the more so be unable to desire or long for it."[7] Thus, even the very *desire* for mystical prayer is strictly *God's gift*. The Catholic mystical tradition is far from the Pelagian heresy that human effort suffices for salvation. (Also, even this is a caricature of what the devout monk Pelagius himself actually wrote.)

Albert Schweitzer, in his controversial 1931 book, *The Mysticism of Paul the Apostle* (which some scholars described as "a book as impressive

6. McGinn, *Mysticism in the Reformation*.

7. Johnston, *The Cloud of Unknowing*, ch. 34, p. 91.

as it is unconvincing"), broke ranks with those scholars who distinguished sharply between pure gospel faith and mysticism. Although I view Schweitzer's book positively, I find his understanding of both Paul and Christian mysticism deficient. For example, he claimed that the mystical charism removed people from ordinary life. Evidently Schweitzer knew nothing of Catherine of Siena, who, during the last five years of her life, was involved in the religio-political problems of the Italian city-states and barely escaped assassination. Highly influential in mitigating the antipapal forces in her region, she also preached in favor of a crusade, the reform of the clergy, and worked for the return of the Avignon papacy to Rome. Her prophetic gifts and letters actually played a role in Pope Gregory XI's decision to move back to Rome. His successor, Urban VI, sought Catherine's support for his legitimacy as pope and called her to Rome in 1379 seeking her help in a vain attempt to win back the schismatics.

Also, were not both John of the Cross and Teresa of Avila deeply involved in the Carmelite Reform that impelled them to both ecclesiastical and political apostolic activity? What of the undeniable apostolic mysticism of St. Ignatius of Loyola, who, as a contemplative in action, found God in all things, established numerous colleges and charitable institutions, and always kept his hand in directly pastoral activity. His thousands of letters demonstrate his far-reaching sociopolitical involvement. Genuine Christian mystics loved the world because God so loved the world. The true Christian mystic loves the so-called ordinary in an extraordinary fashion—the way Jesus-Messiah did and does. Schweitzer also reduced Paul's mysticism to a participation-in-Christ mysticism but denied him other forms of mysticism, especially a God mysticism, because, in his incorrect opinion, this dissolved the difference between God and creature. I shall show later how erroneous Schweitzer's opinion was.

William James has been called the father of twentieth-century American mystical studies and is especially known for his four marks of mystical experience: ineffability, noetic quality, transiency, and passivity.[8] Some commentators have clearly shown that his marks are too broad to be of much use because they can also be used to describe ethical, aesthetic, nature, athletic, and philosophical experiences.[9] Although James correctly maintained that mystical experiences modify the inner life of a person and are transformative,

8. James, *Religious Experience*.

9. Underhill, *Mysticism*, 81–92, offers a much better approach to the marks of genuine Christian mysticism. See, Egan, "Evelyn Underhill Revisited," 223–39.

he neglected to show that Christian mysticism often involves *states* of consciousness that center on the direct and immediate consciousness of God, which becomes a *complete system of life.*

I share James' view of the "strong mystics," such as St. Ignatius of Loyola, whom James praised as one of the most powerful practical human engines that ever lived.[10] However, I reject James' cursory dismissal of the so-called "weak" mystics who do not meet his standards of American pragmatism and self-actualization. He wrote, for example, of one saint this way: "but what were the . . . good fruits from Margaret Mary's life? Apparently little else but suffering, and prayers and absences of mind and swoons and ecstasies; Poor dear sister, indeed! Many other ecstatics would have perished but for the care taken of them by their admiring followers."[11] What would James have said concerning St. Paul's utterance in 2 Corinthians 12:9–10: "But [God] said to me, 'My grace is sufficient for you, for my power is made perfect in weakness.' Therefore I will boast all the more gladly about my weaknesses, so that Christ's power may rest on me. That is why, for Christ's sake, I delight in weaknesses, in insults, in hardships, in persecutions, in difficulties. For when I am weak, then I am strong."

Moreover, what I have called "mystics of reparation," "victim-soul" mystics, and "suffering-servant" mystics permeate the Christian mystical heritage. These so-called "weak" mystics are a lived commentary on three Pauline texts. In 2 Corinthians 5:21, Paul wrote of the sinless Christ who became sin for our salvation. In Colossians 1:24, Paul rejoiced that he was filling up what is lacking in Christ's sufferings. Such mystics understood that they were to incarnate in their lives Christ's social rejection, his failure, his disgrace, his passion, his loneliness and isolation on the cross, and his entombment for the world's salvation. Mystics of reparation were explicitly conscious as "hiding in Christ's wounds," as having his wounds engraved on both their spirits and sometimes their bodies, and living out what St. Paul wrote of himself in Galatians 2:20: "I have been crucified with Christ; it is no longer I who live, but Christ who lives in me."

No person in the Christian mystical tradition has the credentials of Pierre Teilhard de Chardin: Jesuit priest, distinguished member of the French Academy of Science, paleontologist, world traveler, poet, visionary, and mystic. It is difficult to find someone who lived such an intense spiritual and mystical life as Teilhard and yet was so passionately in tune with the secularity of

10. James, *Religious Experience*, 317.

11. James, *Religious Experience*, 268–69.

his era. Intense love for science, the world, and their projects filled his soul. He claimed that because he was a priest, he wished with all his strength to be the first to become aware of what the "world" loves, seeks, and suffers. "I desire," he wrote, "to be . . . the first in self-fulfillment, the first in self-denial—I want to be more widely human in my sympathies and more nobly terrestrial in my ambitions than any of the world's servants."[12]

However, this exceptionally "strong" mystic understood suffering as an evolutionary energy that promotes Christogenesis, the cosmic Christ. In a letter to his invalid sister, Marguerite, he wrote of traveling the world, giving himself "soul and body to the positive forces of the universe," while she was stretched out on her bed of pain, "silently, deep within [herself], transforming into light the world's most grievous shadows. In the eyes of the Creator, which of us will have had the better part?"[13] This is Teilhard's transposition of a suffering-servant mysticism.

In addition, for this missionary to the scientific world, contemplative prayer and purity of heart are also a salient way through which the cosmos is healed, directed, and Christified. He was fond of a story by Robert Hugh Benson in which a visionary enters an out-of-the-way chapel, finds a nun praying, and sees the axis of the universe passing through the chapel and all the elements of the cosmos reorganizing themselves around it. "All at once," Teilhard wrote, "he sees the whole world bound up and moving and organizing itself around that out-of-the way spot, in tune with the intensity and variations of the desires of that puny, praying figure."[14] Because of this nun's contemplative faith and purity of heart, she was an energy center that spearheaded the evolutionary process. Her efficacious and transformative contemplation gave life to, or "sur-animates," the universe. To transpose a Zen saying: the Christian mystic contemplates for the universe.

In addition to William James, who had a profound influence on the course of mystical studies,[15] I shall focus only on the Canadian psychiatrist Richard Maurice Bucke and the British philosopher Walter T. Stace. Bucke's 1901 book, *Cosmic Consciousness: A Study in the Evolution of the Human Mind*, is a compilation of various theories rather than strictly a simple

---

12. Cited in Dumoulin, *Let Me Explain*, 152.

13. Chardin, *Human Energy*, preface.

14. Chardin, *Divine Milieu*, 133.

15. For an excellent summary of the theoretical foundations for the modern study of mysticism, see, McGinn, *The Foundations of Mysticism*, 265–343.

record of his first mystical experience that he had when traveling back to London in a buggy. He later wrote:

> I was in a state of quiet, almost passive enjoyment. All at once, without warning of any kind, I found myself wrapped around as it were by a flame-colored cloud. For an instant I thought of fire, some sudden conflagration in the great city; the next, I knew that the light was within me. Directly afterward came upon me a sense of exultation, of immense joyousness accompanied by an intellectual illumination quite impossible to describe. Into my brain streamed one momentary lightning-flash of the Divine Splendor which has ever since lightened my life; upon my heart fell one drop of Divine Bliss, leaving thenceforward for always an aftertaste of heaven. Among other things, I did not come to believe: I saw and knew that the Cosmos is not dead matter but a living Presence, that the soul of man is immortal, that the universe is so built and ordered that without any peradventure all things work together for the good of each and all, that the foundation principle of the world is what we call love, and that the happiness of everyone in the long run is absolutely certain. I learned more within the few seconds that illumination lasted than in all my previous years of study and I learned much that no study could ever have taught.[16]

He later wrote of the experience's sudden appearance, as an inner light, as moral elevation, as intellectual illumination, as giving a sense of immortality, and as removing the fear of death and the sense of sin. He then wrote:

> This consciousness shows the cosmos to consist not of dead matter governed by unconscious, rigid, and unintending law; it shows it on the contrary as entirely immaterial, entirely spiritual and entirely alive; it shows that death is an absurdity, that everyone and everything has eternal life; it shows that the universe is God and that God is the universe, and that no evil ever did or ever will enter into it; a great deal of this is, of course, from the point of view of self-consciousness, absurd; it is nevertheless undoubtedly true.[17]

Bucke's experience bore only extremely slight similarities to Paul's Damascus-road event and Ignatius' Cardoner episode. Is the universe God? Is it true that evil never entered the universe? In addition, I disagree totally with Bucke's facile application of cosmic consciousness to both Jesus' and Paul's

16. Bucke, *Cosmic Consciousness*, 8–9.
17. Bucke, *Cosmic Consciousness*, 17–18.

life. Moreover, how does one evaluate the judgment of someone who claimed that Walt Whitman was the summit of religious evolution and the herald of humanity's future? The chapters to come will show how different St. Paul's mystical consciousness and life were from Bucke's assessment.

Walter T. Stace influenced many scholars of mysticism, partly because of the dominant scholarly preference for Hindu non-dualistic mysticisms, which emphasize the experience that atman is Brahman—the extreme case being that of the classical Yoga of Patañjali's *samadhi* as the pure, unlimited consciousness of the nothingness of ultimate reality that is viewed as a true death. Thomas Merton understood this when he wrote: "To become a Yogi and to be able to commit moral and intellectual suicide whenever you please, without the necessity of actually dying, to be able to black out your mind by the incantation of half articulate charms and to enter into a state of annihilation, in which all the faculties are inactive and the soul is as inert as if it were dead—all this may well appeal to certain minds as a refined and rather pleasant way of getting even with the world and with society, and with God Himself for that matter."[18]

Stace's highly popular book, *The Teachings of the Mystics*, reduced all mysticism to that of the experience of undifferentiated unity—atman is Brahman—and regarded mysticisms of differentiated unity as "low-level mysticism." He falsely claimed that the mystics of differentiated unity interpret their experiences differently because of theological and ecclesiastical pressure. Not only did he interpret different mystical texts out of context (one scholar called his method that of *philosophical abstraction*) but he also had little knowledge and appreciation of both the *orthodox* Christian undifferentiated-union and the differentiated-union views of many Christian mystics. The positive apophaticism of Jan Ruusbroec is a prime example. Stace also had no knowledge of Christian positive mystical death, as John of the Cross illustrated when he wrote: "I live [in God] not living where I live [on earth]." Moreover, Stace, Bucke, and James wrote nothing about mystical consciousness, states, a transformative life, or experience in the sense of an experienced musician.

Aldous Huxley held the perennial philosophy thesis that all mystical experiences are the same and that even their descriptions reflect an underlying similarity that surpasses religious and cultural diversity.[19] By grounding his notion of mysticism in the structure of human consciousness

18. Merton, "First Christmas at Gethsemane," 30.

19. Huxley, *Doors of Perception*.

as the awareness of the reception of divine love, the Canadian Jesuit phi-losopher-theologian Bernard J. F. Lonergan held the position that all true mysticism, whatever the difference in its mediated content, was essentially the same in the world's major religions.[20]

However, a contemporary mystical theology based on Karl Rahner's distinction between different types of mysticism is much needed.[21] "God-mysticism" purifies, intensifies, and makes more explicit the ever-present, transcendental experience of God. Mysticisms of the "self" (yoga?) heighten and make more transparent the human spirit's "presence to it-self" in every act of consciousness. Rahner emphasizes that one's spirit is unfathomable. Thus, one may plunge into oneself *en*statically and never find anything more than oneself. The spirit, in fact, is so deep that it can engulf one without one ever realizing that there is something further. For example, Martin Buber argued from his own experience for the existence of a "pre-biographical unity of spirit" that supports and subsists beneath all biographical change. He confessed that at first he considered this to be an experience of God but later came to the realization that this was sim-ply the experience of the pre-biographical unity of his own soul.[22] I would also maintain that some yogis seek a type of yogic suicide in which they lose themselves in the experience of the pure, unlimited consciousness of the seeming nothingness of ultimate reality, which is, in fact, only the unlimited openness of the human spirit to infinite reality. For example, I agree with Yves Raguin who wrote: "The important thing here is to realize that my depth is deeper than I am. But at the same time I may plunge into myself and never find anything more than myself. The self, in fact, it is so deep that it can engulf me without me ever realizing that there is some-thing further. . . . It is easy to see why so many mystics lose themselves in themselves and never meet God."[23] In another form of mysticism, namely, nature-mysticism (Zen?), one nourishes the experience of one's pancosmic unity with all creation. Finally, "psychic-mysticisms" make more explicit the experience of one's id and psychic archetypes, of which Shamanism is a prime example. In Rahner's view, psychic mysticisms may account for some of the paranormal phenomena often associated with mysticism.

20. Lonergan, *Method*, esp. 29, 59, 77, 105, 113, 115f., 118, 273.
21. Wong and Egan, *The Christology and Mystical Theology of Karl Rahner.*
22. Buber, *Between Man and Man*, 24.
23. Raguin, *The Depth of God*, 66.

Paul, Christianity's Premier Apostolic Mystic

*"I know a man in Christ who fourteen years ago was
caught up to the third heaven."* (2 Cor 12:2)

As I reread the apostle Paul's epistles in preparation for this book, I thought immediately of two episodes in the life of St. Ignatius of Loyola, the apostolic mystic, which offer an excellent analogy to events in the life of St. Paul, Christianity's premier apostolic mystic. The most important event in Ignatius' life took place on the banks of the river Cardoner, where "the eyes of his understanding began to open and he was infused with a comprehension of many things pertaining to both faith and learning. His understanding was enlightened to such an extent that he thought of himself as if he were another man and that he had an intellect different from the one he had before."[24] Another man! Ignatius the apostolic mystic had been born.

The second salient event took place several years later when Ignatius and two companions, Peter Faber and Diego Laynez, were on their way to Rome to place themselves at the pope's disposal. In a small chapel at La Storta, some six miles north of Rome, Ignatius had a vision of the eternal Father with his cross-bearing Son. Ignatius heard the Father speak interiorly to his heart saying: "I shall be favorable to you [plural] at Rome," and to the Son, "I want you, my Son, to take this man as your servant." Then Jesus said to Ignatius: "I want you [singular] to serve us [Father and Son]."[25] The La Storta graces transformed Ignatius into an apostolic servant—a chosen instrument—with a new heart in the service of God and neighbor, one whose foundational mystical experiences imparted to him a "mystical horizon" in and through which he would later find God in all things.

On the Damascus road, Saul the zealous Pharisee became the new man Paul the zealous Christian apostolic mystic, who would later claim: "have I not seen the Lord" (1 Cor 9:1)—and—"Jesus appeared to me also, as to one abnormally born" (1 Cor 15: 8). Did not Paul write: "I live, not I, but Christ lives in me" (Gal 2:20) and "whoever is united with the Lord is one with him in spirit," a most important text in the Christian mystical tradition? Paul also declared that he had the mind of Jesus-Messiah (1 Cor 2:16) and "took every thought captive to obey him" (2 Cor 10:5)—analogous to Ignatius' new understanding.

24. Ignatius, *Pilgrim's Journey*, nos. 30, 38–39.
25. Rahner, *The Vision in the Chapel of La Storta*, 59–68, my summary.

When Ananias complained to Jesus that Saul had harmed many of Jesus' people in Jerusalem, the Lord replied: "Go! This man is my chosen instrument to proclaim my name to the Gentiles and their kings and to the people of Israel" (Acts 9:15). Both Paul and Ignatius were chosen to be apostolic mystics—in analogous ways, of course. Moreover, Paul wrote of himself several times as a slave of Jesus-Messiah; Ignatius, as a servant of God the Father and his Son. So, I claim that the Damascus road and Cardoner river and La Storta events instilled in both Saul and Ignatius an architectonic, holistic lens—a worldview—and a new mind and heart through which everything else was to be known and loved. Also, did not Jesus explain to the Emmaus disciples "what was said in all the scriptures concerning himself" (Luke 24:27)? Did he not challenge his Jewish opponents: "If you believed Moses, you would believe me, for he wrote about me" (John 5:46)? This illustrates one of the earliest uses of the word "mystical," that is, discovering how Jesus is revealed *in the Jewish scriptures* and underscores how Paul rethought the Jewish scriptures he so loved "in the light of the knowledge of the glory of God in the face of Christ" (2 Cor 4:6).

Paul's mysticism of the cross and resurrection flowed from this light. From this light, Paul consequently mystically reinterpreted the Jewish *Shema*, "Hear, O Israel: The LORD our God, the LORD is one" (Deut 6:4) to include the God-Man Jesus-Messiah and the Holy Spirit. This light also engendered Paul's mysticism of the cross, of the resurrection, of baptism, of the church, of the Eucharist, and of the new creation. Finally, one can also say that in Jesus' light Paul reinterpreted the entire Jewish tradition as fulfilled now in Jesus-Messiah and his Holy Spirit. Salvation is from the Jews. As Paul wrote: "First to the Jew, then to the Gentile" (Rom 1:16). In Paul's view, Christianity is Judaism fulfilled, perfected—not a new religion.

What do the adversaries of Christian mysticism make of 2 Corinthians 12: 2–7, where Paul proclaims:

> I will go on to visions and revelations from the Lord. I know a man in Christ who fourteen years ago was caught up to the third heaven. Whether it was in the body or out of the body I do not know—God knows. And I know that this man—whether in the body or apart from the body I do not know, but God knows—I was caught up to paradise and heard inexpressible things, things that no one is permitted to tell. . . . Even if I should choose to boast, I would not be a fool, because I would be speaking the truth. But I refrain, so no one will think more of me than is warranted by what I do or say, or because of these surpassingly great revelations.

This is the Jewish chariot mysticism of Paul's day, which was heavily influenced by the first chapter of the prophet Ezekiel, which describes a human form above a throne with the appearance of the likeness of the glory of the Lord. When Ezekiel saw it, he fell on his face, and heard the voice of one speaking.

And when one understands Paul's Damascus-road event as seeing God's glory in the face of the risen Jesus-Messiah as mystical, and when one comprehends why Paul wrote of this event as a *revelation* of Jesus-Messiah—the unveiling of secret wisdom that the rulers of this age did not know, not least the revelation of a secret, new type of glory—then one has discovered the primary reason for designating Paul as Christianity's premier apostolic mystic. Did not Paul claim in Galatians 1:11-12 that the gospel he preached was "not of human origin. I did not receive it from any man, nor was I taught it; rather, I received it by revelation from Jesus Christ"? Besides, Paul's magnificent poem in Colossians 1:15-20 assigns to Jesus-Messiah the position one might have expected to be occupied by the Divine Wisdom through which the world was made. It also describes Jesus as the one in whom all the fullness of deity dwells bodily—this, in a sense, is Jewish mysticism that has been redefined and reshaped around Jesus-Messiah. Thus, I maintain that Paul was Christianity's premier apostolic mystic—one who was God-haunted, God-possessed, God-illuminated, and God-transformed—in a trinitarian way—to be the apostle to the gentiles.

In addition to his *visions* of Jesus-Messiah that confirmed his apostolic missions, the following confirms that Paul was also a visionary mystic: "During the night Paul had a vision of a man of Macedonia standing and begging him, 'Come over to Macedonia and help us.' After Paul had seen the vision, we got ready at once to leave for Macedonia, concluding that God had called us to preach the gospel to them" (Acts 16:9-10). The mystical component in Paul's life stands like the central pillar in his entire career. It indicates that one should speak of his mystical life and experience in the sense of an instinctive and holistic way of living and reinterpreting the Jewish scriptures in terms of Jesus-Messiah and the Holy Spirit. Paul's mysticism and his apostolic fervor are two sides of the same coin.

Paul's Mystical Dereliction

"We despaired of life itself." (2 Cor 1:8)

The Christian tradition indicates that the mystical charism inevitably includes phases of profound spiritual and sometimes physical suffering commonly called the dark nights of the spirit and senses. In designating St. Paul as Christianity's premier apostolic mystic, I wish to highlight features of his life that are similar to or at least analogous to the purgative sufferings of the classical mystics.

In relation to the zealous Pharisee Saul, Paul later wrote of himself: "as for righteousness based on the law, blameless" (Phil 3:6).That may be so, but I contend that Saul was also initially blind to his sinful pride, his violent nature, and his psychosomatic disorders. In short, he needed transforming purification and healing, for which the Damascus event was only the initial stage. Did not Jesus say to Ananias about Saul: "I will show him how much he must suffer for my name" (Acts 9:16)? Let me now point to elements in the lives of a few extraordinary mystics and indicate how they apply to Saul the Pharisee who became Paul, Christianity's premier apostolic mystic.

After Ignatius of Loyola's conversion from an often violent life of gambling, dueling, and womanizing, an intense sense of his sinfulness awakened. He feared that no penances would suffice "to give vent to the hatred that he had conceived against himself."[26] Nonetheless, on fire with God, he felt within himself a strong impulse to serve the Lord. For almost a year thereafter, he indulged his thirst for great penances and long hours of prayer. Recovering from his Pamplona battle wounds, he went to Manresa where severe depression, doubts, temptations, and scruples—alternating with great spiritual joys—filled his soul. So painful were the tortures from the scruples about his past sins that Ignatius almost committed suicide. And ill health from the severity of his penances brought him to the brink of death. *I despaired of life itself.*

The sixteenth-century mystic John of the Cross lucidly described the classical characteristics of mystical purgation when he wrote: "this dark night is an inflow of God into the soul, which purges it of its habitual ignorance and imperfections."[27] In John's view, only God can thoroughly purify and increase a person's capacity to love. God's loving inflow into the soul, rather than

---

26. Ignatius, *Pilgrim's Journey*, no. 12, p. 18.

27. John of the Cross, *Dark Night*, Bk. II, chap. 5, no. 1, in *Collected Works*, 335.

causing sweetness and delight, instead produces pain and suffering because of the soul's weakness and sinfulness. As the owl is blinded by gazing into the noonday sun, so the soul is blinded by the flood of God's light and plunged into a bitter "dark night" of purgation. According to this Carmelite's way of thinking, this loving influx, also called infused contemplation, awakens the person not only to his most secret sins and hidden resistance to God but also to his own nothingness and radical distance from God. As purgative, infused contemplation engenders a profound darkness in the soul that seems to dissolve it in a cruel spiritual death, which may bring the contemplative to the brink of physical death. *I despaired of life itself.* The "sorrows of hell" and the feeling of being despised by friends and by all creatures penetrate the contemplative's spirit. The complexity of trials during the dark nights of the spirit and senses is such that John complained that he had neither the time nor the energy to describe their variety and the numerous scriptural passages he could use to illustrate them. Thus, John taught that one may experience many kinds of phenomena during the dark nights.

Marie of the Incarnation, a seventh-century French mystic, had received Jesus' apostolic spirit to become the first woman apostle to North America. She wrote incisively about how the Holy Spirit revealed just how cunning her human nature was in hiding her sins and imperfections.[28] She came to realize that God's light alone could shine into every nook and cranny of her soul to purify, heal, and transform it. The Holy Spirit's presence became "a sword that divided and cut with subtle sharpness," making "subtle" and "penetrating" thrusts into her spirit, which Marie called a "honing purgatory." This applies to Paul. Jesus' Holy Spirit had to awaken him to his dark side.

A salient factor in Paul's difficulties with members of the Corinthian church centered on their desire for a superstar who could brag about his lofty accomplishments and shining charisms. In their view, Paul was deficient: his size (Paul means small), his purported oratorical deficiencies, and his seeming lack of achievements. Paul derisively turned their wish for a celebrity on its head. The first Roman soldier to scale a wall during battle was given a special award for heroism. But Paul wrote: "In Damascus the governor under King Aretas had the city of the Damascenes guarded in order to arrest me. But I was lowered in a basket from a window in the wall and slipped through his hands" (2 Cor 11:32–33). By Roman standards, this was indeed a cowardly act.

28. Marie of the Incarnation, *The Relation of 1654*, 12th state of prayer, LII, 142–43.

Paul also proclaimed:

> Whatever anyone else dares to boast about—I am speaking as
> a fool—I also dare to boast about. Are they Hebrews? So am I.
> Are they Israelites? So am I. Are they Abraham's descendants? So
> am I. Are they servants of Christ? (I am out of my mind to talk
> like this.) I am more. I have worked much harder, been in prison
> more frequently, been flogged more severely, and been exposed
> to death again and again. Five times I received from the Jews
> the forty lashes minus one. Three times I was beaten with rods,
> once I was pelted with stones, three times I was shipwrecked, I
> spent a night and a day in the open sea, I have been constantly
> on the move. I have been in danger from rivers, in danger from
> bandits, in danger from my fellow Jews, in danger from Gentiles;
> in danger in the city, in danger in the country, in danger at sea;
> and in danger from false believers. I have labored and toiled and
> have often gone without sleep; I have known hunger and thirst
> and have often gone without food; I have been cold and naked.
> Besides everything else, I face daily the pressure of my concern
> for all the churches. Who is weak, and I do not feel weak? Who
> is led into sin, and I do not inwardly burn? If I must boast, I will
> boast of the things that show my weakness.

Jesus-Messiah had told Ananias how much Paul would have to suffer
to proclaim his name. When one contemporary bishop quoted this text,
he quipped that wherever he goes—and he emphasized his comfortable
modes of transportation—there were banquets, not riots and beatings, as
happened to Paul.

Even in 1 Corinthians 4:9–13, where the mood is lighter and less
ironic, we find Paul stating the same theme:

> For it seems to me that God has put us apostles on display at the
> end of the procession, like those condemned to die in the arena.
> We have been made a spectacle to the whole universe, to angels
> as well as to human beings. We are fools for Christ, but you are so
> wise in Christ! We are weak, but you are strong! You are honored,
> we are dishonored! To this very hour we go hungry and thirsty,
> we are in rags, we are brutally treated, we are homeless. We work
> hard with our own hands. When we are cursed, we bless; when we
> are persecuted, we endure it; when we are slandered, we answer
> kindly. We have become the scum of the earth, the garbage of the
> world—right up to this moment.

No wonder Paul boasted in Galatians 6:17: "From now on, let no one cause me trouble, for I bear on my body the marks of Jesus." Certainly Paul's body bore the scars from his numerous beating, floggings, and stonings. Some scholars speculate that, like Francis of Assisi, Paul was, in fact, stigmatic. Slaves and soldiers were branded and Paul declared himself to be a slave of Jesus-Messiah. He also wrote that he had been crucified with Jesus-Messiah and now lived Jesus-Messiah's own crucified and risen, suffering and glorious life.

When Paul returned to the subject in his Second Letter to the Corinthians, the mood has changed: he wrote about his troubles in Asia, where he was so utterly, unbearably crushed that he despaired of life itself and felt that he had received the death sentence (2 Cor 1:8–9). He had been so crushed, devastated by events, which he does not describe, that he gave up on life itself: the classic symptoms of deep depression. Writing as one who had looked into the pit, he was surprised that he had not fallen in. Thus, while depression and the mystical dereliction are similar symptoms of a fragmented identity, from the standpoint of prognosis they differ. In other words, this was Paul's deep experience of the dark night of the spirit.

Of course, God had never abandoned Paul and on several occasions Jesus-Messiah and also a "night angel" had appeared to strengthen him. In Acts 18:9–11, we read: "One night the Lord spoke to Paul in a vision: 'Do not be afraid; keep on speaking, do not be silent. For I am with you, and no one is going to attack and harm you, because I have many people in this city.'" Acts 27:23–24 relates: "The following night the Lord stood near Paul and said, 'Take courage! As you have testified about me in Jerusalem, so you must also testify in Rome,'" and in Acts 27: 23–24: "Last night an angel of the God to whom I belong and whom I serve stood beside me and said, 'Do not be afraid, Paul. You must stand trial before Caesar; and God has graciously given you the lives of all who sail with you.'"

What Luke wrote about Paul in Acts 16:16–23 is indicative of Paul's many ordeals:

> Once when we were going to the place of prayer, we were met by a slave woman who had a spirit by which she predicted the future. She earned a great deal of money for her owners by fortune-telling. She followed Paul and the rest of us, shouting, "These men are servants of the Most High God, who are telling you the way to be saved." She kept this up for many days. Finally Paul became so annoyed that he turned around and said to the spirit, "In the name of Jesus Christ I command you to come out of her!" At that moment

the spirit left her. When her owners realized that their hope of making money was gone, they seized Paul and Silas and dragged them into the marketplace to face the authorities. They brought them before the magistrates and said, "These men are Jews, and are throwing our city into an uproar by advocating customs unlawful for us Romans to accept or practice." The crowd joined in the attack against Paul and Silas, and the magistrates ordered them to be stripped and beaten with rods. After they had been severely flogged, they were thrown into prison, and the jailer was commanded to guard them carefully.

Thus, in Philippi, Paul's exorcism of a slave woman ruined business for the owners who said that he was teaching Jewish customs illegal under Roman law. Anyone who has been attacked by a mob, flogged, and thrown into prison knows what Paul must have experienced and thought. More importantly, here is a spiritual battle with economic consequences framed as a religious problem with political implications.

In Thessalonica Paul was accused of sedition by proclaiming that there was another king: Jesus-Messiah (Acts 17:1–9). Once again, Paul's action caused a mob to form, a riot, and turmoil. In one place after another, he horrified many Jews with his message of a crucified Messiah and his proclamation that this Messiah was now welcoming non-Jews without circumcision. This inevitably led to opposition, at times intensified by local hostility from gentiles who may have had no special sympathy for the Jewish people, but who saw Paul as a social and cultural threat. Thus, opposition was sometimes aroused because pagans saw him as a dangerous kind of Jew. At times, it was because Jews saw him as flirting dangerously with paganism.

The massive temple of fertility goddess Artemis at Ephesus possessed imposing power because of imperial cult. So the local silversmiths had the same problem with Paul as the slaveowners did in Philippi, only much more so. Luke relates in Acts 19:23–30:

> About that time there arose a great disturbance about the Way. A silversmith named Demetrius, who made silver shrines of Artemis, brought in a lot of business for the craftsmen there. He called them together, along with the workers in related trades, and said: "You know, my friends, that we receive a good income from this business. And you see and hear how this fellow Paul has convinced and led astray large numbers of people here in Ephesus and in practically the whole province of Asia. He says that gods made by human hands are no gods at all. There is danger not only that our

trade will lose its good name, but also that the temple of the great goddess Artemis will be discredited; and the goddess herself, who is worshiped throughout the province of Asia and the world, will be robbed of her divine majesty." When they heard this, they were furious and began shouting: "Great is Artemis of the Ephesians!" Soon the whole city was in an uproar. The people seized Gaius and Aristarchus, Paul's traveling companions from Macedonia, and all of them rushed into the theater together. Paul wanted to appear before the crowd, but the disciples would not let him.

Here Paul denounced the great goddess herself, telling people that gods made with hands were not gods at all. Thus, we find Paul causing a riot because he threatened the livelihood of the silversmiths and blasphemed Artemis. However, here, just as in Thessalonica or Athens, the primary impact of Paul's message was not how to be saved, though that was part of it, nor even that the Messiah died for your sins. The announcement of the crucified and risen Messiah itself only made sense within the larger picture of the one God. It was essentially a Jewish message confronting a world full of false gods with the news of the living one. Contemporary popular consciousness has no idea how important the Romans and Greeks considered their gods to be in upholding political, economic, and agricultural life and how quickly and thoroughly Christianity destroyed idolatry.[29]

It was not just pagan hostility that landed Paul where he was. (I agree with those scholars who contend that Paul was imprisoned twice in Ephesus.) Even the local people whom he considered as friends turned out to be his enemies or at least rivals. One way or another Paul found himself in prison, on a charge that might very easily have meant death. I suspect that Paul interpreted his imprisonment in Ephesus as the revenge of the dark powers into whose world he had been making inroads. He was used to confronting synagogue authorities. He knew how to deal with Roman magistrates. He knew Jewish and Roman law just as well as they did. But in this case he had sensed that something else was going on. The dark forces arranged against him were not simply human. Did he not write in Ephesians 6:11–12: "Put on the full armor of God, so that you can take your stand against the devil's schemes. For our struggle is not against flesh and blood, but against the rulers, against the authorities, against the powers of this dark world and against the spiritual forces of evil in the heavenly realms"?

29. Hurtado, *Destroyer of the Gods.*

Paul's impressive ministry in Ephesus stirred up a hornets nest. The many magic books being burned would have certainly awakened "the powers of this dark world" to Paul's power with the gospel of Jesus-Messiah. Jesus had warned his followers not to fear those who could merely kill the body, but rather to fear the dark powers that could bring about a more horrible destruction. Just as Jesus had understood himself ushering in the kingdom by definitively defeating the "strong man" (Mark 3:22–30), so Paul was learning that human authorities might sometimes be acting merely as a front for other dark powers that would attack through them.[30] The desert fathers often regarded themselves as "demon wrestlers" and the Christian mystical tradition is replete with those who knew that their mystical journey would involve doing battle with Satan and his minions.[31]

Although Paul had taught, preached, and celebrated the fact that Jesus' death had defeated all the dark powers and that in his resurrection he had launched God's new creation, that unflinching belief, seen from the cold, stinking depths of a hell-hole prison, with no lights at night, flies and vermin for company, and little food in his stomach, must have been tested to the uttermost and beyond. *I despaired of life itself.* I would argue that, like a plant in harsh winter, Paul in prison was forced to put his roots down even deeper than he had yet gone into the biblical tradition, and deeper again, still within that tradition, into the meaning of Jesus-Messiah's life death and resurrection. However, Paul never gave up and wrote: "But we have this treasure in jars of clay to show that this all-surpassing power is from God and not from us. We are hard pressed on every side, but not crushed; perplexed, but not in despair; persecuted, but not abandoned; struck down, but not destroyed. We always carry around in our body the death of Jesus, so that the life of Jesus may also be revealed in our body" (2 Cor 4:7–10). And the poems of Philippians 2, Colossians 1, and the sustained liturgical drama of the first three chapters of Ephesians, all bear witness to the celebration of God's victory and Jesus-Messiah's Lordship.

What did Paul think about during his trials, especially during his three imprisonments, during his being adrift at sea, his sleepless nights, the satanic thorn in his flesh, which many scholars think is a biblical way of saying enemies within one's own community, and so on? His remembrance of his persecution of the church, his deadliest sin, mentioned eight times in the New Testament, must have tortured him—as well as a growing awareness of

30. Egan, *Christian Mysticism*, 347–52.
31. Egan, *Sounding.*

his hidden sins. One find this torment as well as Jesus-Messiah's commissioning him to be an apostle to the gentiles clearly in Acts 22:17–21:

> When I [Paul] returned to Jerusalem and was praying at the temple, I fell into a trance and saw the Lord speaking to me. "Quick!" he said. "Leave Jerusalem immediately, because the people here will not accept your testimony about me." "Lord," I replied, "these people know that I went from one synagogue to another to imprison and beat those who believe in you. And when the blood of your martyr Stephen was shed, I stood there giving my approval and guarding the clothes of those who were killing him." Then the Lord said to me, "Go; I will send you far away to the Gentiles."

He must have asked if God had abandoned him and why those closest to him—his family and friends—had turned against him. Notice how even Jesus' family thought that he was out of his mind (Mark 3:21) for proclaiming that the kingdom of God had come in his person. Likewise, it was not only King Agrippa who thought that Paul was insane (Acts 26:24). N. T. Wright suggests that when Paul returned from his journeys, his family and possibly a fiancée thought him insane because of his proclamation of a crucified and risen Messiah.[32] As the many mystics after him experienced, Paul knew firsthand the deep pain of rejection, not only from strangers, but also from those closest to him.

Paul wrote the seemingly strange statement: "I am not ashamed of the gospel" (Rom 1:16). Remember, however, that Jews and gentiles ridiculed the notion of a crucified Messiah. Paul was an apostle proclaiming a message that brought him regular shame and ridicule.

Romans 9:1-4 bears witness to another great source of Paul's suffering: "I speak the truth in Christ—I am not lying, my conscience confirms it through the Holy Spirit—I have great sorrow and unceasing anguish in my heart. For I could wish that I myself were cursed and cut off from Christ for the sake of my people, those of my own race, the people of Israel." Jesus' own people had turned their backs on him. To be sure, he could later say: "therefore, having this ministry by the mercy of God, we do not lose heart" (2 Cor 4:1).

This long list of Paul's sufferings for the sake of his apostolate clearly highlights his mystical dereliction as Christianity's premier apostolic mystic and a fulfillment of what Jesus had told Ananias. "I will show him how much he must suffer for my name." *I despaired of life itself.*

32. Wright, *Paul: A Biography*, 77–83.

Chapter 3

Paul's Mysticism of the Cross
and Resurrection

Paul's Mysticism of the Cross

*"May I never boast except in the cross of
our Lord Jesus Christ."* (Gal 6:14)

THE CRUCIFIXION OF JESUS-MESSIAH is the most important event in history. The second-century bishop Melito of Sardis proclaimed: "He was raised on the cross. He who fixed the heavens is fixed to the wood. God is murdered!"[1] N. T. Wright's correctly focuses on Jesus' crucifixion as the day the revolution began.[2] Of all history's victims who were crucified in the Roman era, Jesus of Nazareth is the one known to us by name.

The Pharisee Saul met the risen Christ on the Damascus road, which made him an apostle. Later, this man in Christ was taken up to the third heaven and into paradise (2 Cor 12:2). Therefore, is it not paradoxical that Paul rejoiced in his weakness and the cross to write: "For I resolved to know nothing while I was with you except Jesus Christ and him crucified" (1 Cor 12:2)? This underscores the heart of Paul's mysticism of the cross. And because Paul will reflect in detail on the significance of Jesus' crucifixion and unbelievers' ridicule, a summary overview of the shocking indignities that lead to the death of Jesus is here first outlined."

Jesus' claim to be definitively inaugurating the kingdom of God— verified by his miraculous cures, exorcisms, raising Lazarus from the dead, as well as his predictions against the temple and the Jewish people—had

1. Cited in Rutledge, *The Crucifixion*, vii.
2. Wright, *The Day the Revolution Began.*

made him a key enemy of Jewish authorities. Because of Jesus' kingdom proclamations and the many Jewish revolutionaries plotting to overthrow the Romans, they, too, would have been suspicious of yet another would-be messianic troublemaker.

Thus, the Jews demanded that Pontius Pilate execute Jesus by crucifixion—the Roman way of turning their worst enemies into excrement. And because of the Book of Deuteronomy's proclamation that he who hangs upon a tree is cursed (Deut 21:23), Jewish eyes would have viewed the crucified Jesus-Messiah as God-cursed excrement. In accordance with the text from Deuteronomy, which Paul quoted, he wrote: "Christ redeemed us from the curse of the law" (Gal 3:13). Paul furthered declared to the Corinthians that God made Jesus—who had no sin—to be sin for us (2 Cor 5:21). Thus, the sheer godlessness and horror of the cross because by it Jesus was both cursed and sin itself—seemingly utterly defeated. Satanic evil, Israel's evil, the entire history of human evil, our evil, murdered the Way, the Truth, and the Life—the God-Man himself. This is a saturated phenomenon replete with inexhaustible meaning.[3]

The Romans had perfected the most gruesome form of execution ever invented. In the first phase, the naked victim was scourged with whips that tore flesh from his back and buttocks. Throughout the night, the Roman soldiers would have delighted in sexually shaming and abusing Jesus, a Jewish circumcised prisoner. Also, crowned with thorns and donning a purple robe, Jesus-Messiah the king would have been ridiculed, taunted, mocked, and spit upon: a ritual of total infamy.

Roman soldiers were highly skilled at driving the nails just close enough to the radial nerves to cause violent bolts of pain when the cross was lifted, and whenever the victim attempted to move. Because the crucified could breathe only if he moved, thus intensifying his pain, in a sense he killed himself by suffocation. In addition, the unspeakably thirsty crucified person was usually naked, unable to control bodily functions, and tormented by carrion birds and insects feasting on open wounds—all adding to his humiliation and suffering. This excruciation could last several days. The crucified were purposely made a public spectacle, a billboard, a sign of warning: "do not mess with the Romans." Exposed to the full scorn of spectators, Jesus-Messiah would have been subjected to their verbal abuse and to their throwing of whatever objects and filth were at hand. Death by crucifixion was so vile and horrendous that it was against the law to crucify

---

3. The best book on this theme is Rutledge, *Crucifixion*.

a Roman citizen—undoubtedly why Paul, a Roman citizen—was probably beheaded, and not crucified. Even the word was not uttered in polite Roman society. Jews would have found crucifixion even more abhorrent because of its association with God's curse. The Qur'an simply denies that Allah would have allowed the prince of peace to be crucified.

Christ crucified—a pitiable, twisted, contorted, shuddering of a man, a comic gargoyle—was the suffering servant prophesied by Isaiah and Psalm 22: "I am a worm and no man." How the apostle Paul and the early Christians must have been ridiculed when they preached a crucified Messiah. This is behind Paul's strange words: "I am not ashamed of the gospel" (Rom 1:16).

This subversive symbol is so contradictory that rock stars and celebrities display it as non-religious jewelry. Many companies prohibit their employees from wearing it so as not to offend customers. Even Nike or McDonald's does not have such an ubiquitous logo! However, the cross has become domesticated, made routine, and respectable. To portray the sufferings of women, British artist Edwina Sandys molded *Christa*, a four-foot, nude crucified female Christ that hung in New York's Cathedral Church of St. John the Divine, which was soon taken down because of a severe backlash. One pastor upset his parishioners by placing a statue of Jesus in an electric chair in the parish church. However, even the electric chair is a far cry from one of history's most vile, horrendous, and *public* instruments of death: the cross.

Yet, Paul clearly did not view the cross as an embarrassment but as something to *boast* about. Why? Because he understood the cross as the mysterious key to the meaning of God, life, the world, and human destiny. He knew all along that the Creator had made the world out of overflowing, generous love. Therefore, the spilling over, the self-sacrificial love of the crucified Son was the genuine self-expression of God's love for a world radically out of joint and his way of putting it right. Paul's mysticism of the cross underscored God's love ushering in God's kingdom *on earth* as it is in heaven. Are not the wordless groanings of the Holy Spirit in Romans 8 part of what it means to be God—to be both present in the depths of the world's pain and transcendent over it, and searching all hearts? In addition, both Jesus' cry of dereliction on the cross and the Holy Spirit's groaning are essential elements in the very identity of the God of superabundant love.

Paul warned the Ephesian Christians that "our struggle is not against flesh and blood, but against the rulers, against the authorities, against the powers of this dark world and against the spiritual forces of evil in the heavenly realms" (Eph 6:12). And struggle he did. However, because of Paul's mysticism of the cross, he declared to the Colossians: "And having disarmed the powers and authorities, [Jesus-Messiah] made a public spectacle of them, triumphing over them by the cross" (Col 2:15). In Paul's view, the cross possessed revolutionary power—God's very own power. It had everything to do with the forgiveness of sins, but also with social and political evil and with Christ's victory over Satan and his cronies. He could mockingly announce: "No, we declare God's wisdom, a mystery that has been hidden and that God destined for our glory before time began. None of the rulers of this age understood it, for if they had, they would not have crucified the Lord of glory" (1 Cor 2:7–8), and thus signed their own death warrant.

Paul announced to the Galatians that, according to the will of God the Father, Jesus-Messiah gave himself for our sins to rescue us in the present evil age (Gal 1:3-4). This fulfillment of God's age-old plan brought about the new Passover, the new exodus, liberation from enslaving demonic powers, and the completion of Israel's God-drenched history. This may account for the puzzling fact that the central belief of the early Christians focused neither on Jesus' crucifixion nor his bodily resurrection but on his descent into hell.[4] An intrinsic connection definitely exists between Paul's emphasis on the crucified Jesus-Messiah as "God's power and wisdom" (1 Cor 1: 22–24)[5] and Jesus' victorious descent into hell.[6] Yet, despite its inclusion in the Apostles Creed, Christ's descent into hell remains a mostly ignored belief.

The church fathers understood that the gates of heaven were closed until Christ's victorious death on the cross. The just who died before this event were in a holding pattern in the limbo of the fathers, a place of refreshment (the *refrigerium*), until Jesus-Messiah's victory. Other fathers, on the basis of 1 Peter 3:18–22 ("He was put to death in the body but made alive in the Spirit. After being made alive, he went and made proclamation to the imprisoned spirits—to those who were disobedient long ago when God waited patiently in the days of Noah while the ark was being built. In it only a few people, eight in all, were saved through water, and this

4. The most important contemporary studies on Christ's descent into hell is Pitstick, *Christ's Descent* and *Light in Darkness*. The vast number of liturgical and theological interpretations as well as quantity of artistic and iconic depictions throughout Christian history on this creedal statement is dizzying.

5. For an excellent, contemporary interpretation of this topic, see Walter Wink's trilogy, *Powers*.

6. Rutledge, *Crucifixion*, chaps. 9–10, 348–461.

water symbolizes baptism that now saves you also"), 1 Peter 4:6, Romans 10:7, and the non-Pauline Epistle to the Hebrews 13:20, claimed that Christ preached the good news and baptized them. Contemporary scholars tend to reduce the creedal statement of Christ's descent into hell as meaning simply that he died and was buried, sharing the same fate all humans do. Contemporary liberation theologians stress that Jesus' baptism indicates his solidarity and identification with all humanity—his descent into hell, his solidarity with the dead, the forgotten, the victims of tyranny, slavery, injustice, the utterly silent and forgotten of history. Consonant with this is the thinking of the German theologian Johann Baptist Metz (d. 2019), who emphasized the importance of "dangerous memory" in regard to this forgotten history.[7] Joseph Ratzinger (later as Pope Benedict XVI) held that Jesus' descent into hell was a modality of his victorious resurrection.

Paul hints at this doctrine when we wrote: "'Who will descend into the deep?' (that is, to bring Christ up from the dead)" (Rom 10:7) and "What does 'he ascended' mean except that he also descended to the lower, earthly regions" (Eph 4:9)? We can also see it hinted at because of the book of Deuteronomy's proclamation that he who hangs upon a tree is cursed (Deut 21:23), which Paul quoted, he wrote: "Christ redeemed us from the curse of the law" (Gal 3:13). Paul furthered declared to the Corinthians that God made Jesus—who had no sin—to be sin for us (2 Cor 5:21). Thus, consonant with Paul, I maintain that a salient aspect of the crucified Messiah's victory was his descent into hell, because on the cross he performed his definitive exorcism by entering Satan's domain of Death and Sin to destroy it. As Jesus said: "In fact, no one can enter a strong man's house without first tying him up. Then he can plunder the strong man's house" (Mark 3:27). Consonant with this is the view of the author of the Epistle to the Hebrews who wrote: "Since the children have flesh and blood, [Jesus-Messiah] too shared in their humanity so that by his death he might break the power of him who holds the power of death—that is, the devil—and free those who all their lives were held in slavery by their fear of death" (Heb 2:14–15). Paul's writings indicate at least implicitly that he saw the link between the principalities and powers, sin, and death.

Thus, I do not share the views of the German Reformed theologian and Professor Emeritus of Systematic Theology at the University of Tübingen, Jürgen Moltmann, who argued that Jesus' death caused a rupture between him and his Father with their unity being secretly sustained by the Holy

7. Metz, *Faith in History and Society.*

Spirit.[8] Hans Urs von Balthasar contended that during the crucifixion, Jesus lost his identity to become metaphysical sin (whatever that is), the Father changed into blazing wrath against sin, while the Holy Spirit preserved the unity between Father and Son.[9]

Rejecting the gnostic views of both Moltmann and Balthasar, I prefer to understand Jesus' descent into hell not only as one aspect of his victorious definitive exorcism on the cross but also as his psychological sufferings, both in the Garden of Olives and on the cross. In becoming sin and cursed by God, Jesus-Messiah experienced the dereliction many mystics underwent. Let me give two example: Hadewijch and Camilla Battista da Varano.

Hadewijch, the majestic but until recently undeservedly neglected thirteenth-century mystic-Beguine, wrote in her sixteenth poem in couplets of Love's seven names: a chain, a light, a live coal, fire, dew, living, and finally: "Hell," however, "is Love's highest name. No grace exists there because this insurmountable darkness of Love engulfs and damns everything."[10] Perhaps a more poignant statement of mystical dereliction cannot be found in the mystical tradition.

One of the most fascinating mystical autobiographies ever written, *The Spiritual Life*, flowed from the pen of the Italian mystic nun Camilla Battista da Varano (1458–1524).[11] The inner sufferings that had consumed her for three years compelled her to write her book, the final chapters (XVII–XIX) of which contain one of the most profound descriptions of the hellish state of mystical dereliction ever written. While being submerged in what she described as God's deep and profound sea, she became conscious of three paradoxes that left her in despair and drove her to the bottom of a hell filled with the "envenomed dragon of the abyss." Her teaching: God *is* hell to sinful human beings. However, as seen in Hadewijch's life, Love itself can be experienced as hell, even for those highly advanced in the mystical life. I tentatively maintain that Jesus-Messiah's death on the cross was both a defeat and a victory, the experience of the full weight of sin and being cursed by God—thus, descending into hell—but also a victory, in the sense of having bound the "strong man," and of anticipating

---

8. Moltmann *The Crucified God*.

9. Pitstick, *Theology of Holy Saturday*. Her tables (ibid., 26–28, 53–58, 73, 83–84) and the five appendices (ibid., 113–30) provide a brilliant summary of various positions on this difficult topic.

10. *Hadewijch: Poems in Couplets*, 16, no. 45, 353; no. 85, 354.

11. McGinn, *Vernacular Mysticism*, 306–11.

his resurrection. Did not Jesus say both "My God, my God, why have you forsaken me" (Mark 15:34) but also "when I am lifted up from the earth, [I] will draw all people to myself" (John 12:32)?

Some of Paul's epistles recount the two stories of Adam and of Israel, weaving them together to show—as can be found in much Jewish tradition—just how closely they resonate with one another. Paul believed that through the Torah Israel brought Adam's sin to completion. Thus, he referred to SIN[12] as a power, a force, a domain, fully developed, and doing its worst. SIN was the cumulation not only of human wrongdoings but also of the powers unleashed by idolatry and wickedness—the power that humans were supposed to have, but that through idolatry they handed over to pseudo-gods. The word SIN is a personification and another word for the serpent in Genesis, SATAN, and DEATH.

Paul stressed that the one who died was Israel's Messiah. He understood the larger storyline of Adam and Abraham, of Moses, of the monarchy, and of the extended exile in terms of Jesus-Messiah. If one fails to see Paul's comprehension of Jesus as Israel's Messiah, then one will never understand what Paul realized had taken place in Jesus-Messiah's crucifixion. Paul's mysticism of the cross focused on the cross as the dramatic and shocking resolution of the biblical narrative. The cross had created a new world in which those who are grasped by Jesus' crucifixion have a whole new set of tasks opening up before them. In telling the story this way, Paul resolutely located the deepest meaning of the cross within Israel's narrative. That is where it should remain. Taken out of that story, it becomes a quasi-pagan tale that separates Jesus' crucifixion from the love of the Creator God for Israel and the world.

Paul maintained that God's eternal purpose was attained by means of Jesus' death on the cross, through which the power of SIN, SATAN, and DEATH were defeated. Jesus-Messiah, representing Israel and the world, took upon himself the full force of the divine condemnation of sin itself, so that all those in him would not suffer it themselves. This substitution theory[13] finds its true meaning within the narrative of Israel's God-given covenant and vocation to be the light of the world. Salvation is from the Jews, as Jesus said. Paul emphasized the cross as the power of

12. I am purposely using Rutledge's capitalization of SIN, SATAN, and DEATH for emphasis. It also highlights Paul's view of them as a domain.

13. Substitutionary atonement—briefly and much oversimplified—means that Christ suffered for us or was punished instead of us.

God that brings salvation to everyone who believes: first to the Jew, then to the gentile (Rom 1:16). In Romans 11:1, Paul asked: "did God reject his people? By no means! I am an Israelite myself, a descendant of Abraham. God did not reject his people, whom he foreknew." As the Israelites were freed from Egyptian slavery, humans are rescued in order to be glorified and according to the Spirit—but now no longer according to the flesh. Humans were ransomed not so that they can go to heaven but so that the right and proper verdict of the law can be fulfilled in them. Only then can we have genuine human existence, as bearers of the divine image, and reflect God's wisdom and love into the world.

Paul insisted that it was God's purpose to allow the Torah to heap up sin in this way. It was God's Son, his second self, who was sent in the likeness of sinful flesh. It was God's love that was expressed in action, as Paul insisted in Romans 5:8: "But God demonstrates his own love for us in this: While we were still sinners, Christ died for us." Paul grasped the death of Jesus as the ultimate expression of divine love, that covenantal love that lay at the heart of so many ancient Israelite expressions of hope for covenant rescue and renewal. Thus, in the sending of the Son, YHWH, the Creator and covenant God, sent his very own self. Much contemporary thinking errs when it assumes that God the Father wrathfully willed his Son's suffering and death—almost as a form of child abuse. To Paul's way of thinking, God the Father willed Jesus-Messiah's life of goodness and love that would smoke out evil and conquer it on the cross. God the Father willed the end of the slavery wrought on Israel and the world through SATAN, SIN, and DEATH, which Paul understood as all linked.

In Romans 8:3–4 Paul maintained that "what the law was powerless to do because it was weakened by the flesh, God did by sending his own Son in the likeness of sinful flesh to be a sin offering. And so he condemned sin in the flesh." N. T. Wright wrote:

> Paul does not . . . say that "God condemned Jesus." He says, rather, that "God condemned sin in the flesh of his son." That makes a considerable difference. . . . But the punishment, here at least, is not so much the punishment that "I" deserve, but the punishment that "sin" deserved. . . . It is the horrifying realization, in the light of the fact of the crucified Messiah, that Israel was called to be the place where "sin would be condemned in the flesh"—and that the Messiah has taken that role unto himself, individually.[14]

14. Wright, *Faithfulness of God*, 898.

Thus, Paul proclaimed that God punished SIN in Jesus' flesh. Of course, this did not alleviate the physical, mental, spiritual agony and death that Jesus endured. Seen in this light, the death of Jesus is certainly penal. But it has to do with the punishment on *SIN*, not, to repeat, on Jesus—but it is punishment nonetheless. God the Father condemned SIN in the flesh of the Messiah. The one dies and the many do not.

God used the cross to reveal our sin and thus destroy the power that Satan has over us when our sin is kept in the dark. Obviously the Scriptures and the early church fathers—but not Paul—also use the language of "payment" in describing what Jesus' blood does for our sin. However, where this concept of "payment" is fleshed out, it is a ransom payment to the slave-master Satan rather than a debt payment to a moral banker God. As Paul underscored: "Don't you know that when you offer yourselves to someone as obedient slaves, you are slaves of the one you obey—whether you are slaves to sin, which leads to death, or to obedience, which leads to righteousness? . . . You have been set free from sin and have become slaves to righteousness. . . . Just as you used to offer yourselves as slaves to impurity and to ever-increasing wickedness, so now offer yourselves as slaves to righteousness leading to holiness" (Rom 6:16–19). Thus, in this chapter Paul wrote about our emancipation from our slavery to sin as a change of masters in which righteousness becomes our new master.

What Plato wrote in his work, *The Republic*, some four centuries before Jesus-Messiah, sheds light on Jesus' crucifixion: "the perfectly just man will have to be scourged, racked, fettered, blinded, and then after the most extreme suffering, he will be crucified."[15] Consonant with Plato is the view of the English-born Irish Dominican priest, theologian, and philosopher, Herbert McCabe, who wrote: "if you love effectively, you will be killed."[16]

I find the following analogy helpful for understanding the Father's role in relation to his crucified Son. During the Chernobyl nuclear disaster, a Russian Air Force general sent his helicopter-pilot son into harm's way. The pilots who covered the reactor with sand and cement faced a certain and gruesome death from radiation. That Russian general, a father, certainly did not want his son to die—but to save others. Thus, contrary to popular views, it is not that the triune God was angry with humankind, Jesus-Messiah dies on cross, and then God becomes our friend again— as if the crucifixion changes God. God is eternal love and certainly not

15. Plato, *The Republic*, 361e–362e.
16. McCabe, *God Still Matters*, 92–101.

guilty of divine child abuse, as some thinkers write. In the stunning words of the apostle Paul:

> [God] chose us in him before the creation of the world to be holy and blameless in his sight. In love predestined us for adoption to sonship through Jesus Christ, in accordance with his pleasure and will—to the praise of his glorious grace, which he has freely given us in the One he loves. In him we have redemption through his blood, the forgiveness of sins, in accordance with the riches of God's grace that he lavished on us. (Eph 1:4–9)

Did not the apostle Paul write:

> For the creation was subjected to frustration, not by its own choice, but by the will of the one who subjected it, in hope that the creation itself will be liberated from its bondage to decay and brought into the freedom and glory of the children of God. We know that the whole creation has been groaning as in the pains of childbirth right up to the present time. Not only so, but we ourselves, who have the first fruits of the Spirit, groan inwardly as we wait eagerly for our adoption to sonship, the redemption of our bodies. (Rom 8:20–23)

How many Christians realize the *cosmic* nature of Christ's descent into hell through his death on the cross? In line with Paul, Karl Rahner wrote of the crucified Jesus-Messiah as

> inserted into this whole world in its ground as a permanent determination of a real ontological kind. . . . To the innermost reality of the world there belongs what we call Jesus Christ in his life and death, what was poured out over the cosmos at the moment when the vessel of his body was shattered in death, and Christ became, even in his humanity, what he had always been by his dignity, the heart of the universe, the innermost center of all created reality.[17]

Although Rahner used the word *world*, he used the term analogously to mean *cosmos,* a term the quotation contains. Jesus' apocalyptic victory reached and transformed every dimension of creation: earth, heaven, hell, past, present, and future—all this, as Paul wrote, by Christ "making peace through his blood, shed on the cross" (Col 1:20).

Paul's Epistle to the Romans also proclaimed that we have been justified—set straight—by Christ's blood (Rom 5:9). As a result of this

---

17. Rahner, "A Faith That Loves the Earth," 332.

justification, Jesus rescued believers from the wrath caused by sin. Paul's mysticism centered on Jesus' blood may have arisen from his appreciation of Jewish peace offerings, which in the Jewish scriptures do *not* depict an angry pagan god demanding sacrifice to change his mind. After the priest killed an animal, its blood, the symbol of life, was poured on the altar—the place where heaven and earth meet. This rite highlights that all life belongs God. The blood was then sprinkled on the people to stress that life is God's gift to his people. The *blood*, not the killing of the animal, removed the people's sins. Some of the meat was given to the priest and the rest eaten by the people in a communal meal—a foreshadowing of the Christian Eucharistic meal-sacrifice.

Of course, blood is a symbol of life, and for many Christian mystics, blood is love made visible. In the context of the peace offering, it emphasizes the one blood, the one life, shared between God and his people. In some movies, two men slit their hands to mingle blood to become blood brothers. In the bar scene of the movie *The Indian Runner*, the good brother slits his hand with a broken beer bottle, shows his evil brother the blood, and says: "family here or stay in this hell of a bar." I suggest that Paul interpreted the shedding of Jesus-Messiah's blood along these lines.

With respect to Paul's writing about wrath, a striking mural in a charming Austrian village Catholic church shows the crucified Christ restraining the sword arm of a wrathful God the Father—with Mary holding up her mantel of protection—with the world and its people behind it. This mural depicts what many Christians falsely believe: God the Father wishes us damned; the Son wishes our salvation. Yes, the New Testament does speak of God's anger, judgment, justice, sword, and wrath approximately forty-six times. However, I suspect that the great fifteenth-century mystic Julian of Norwich's firm conviction that a Trinity of love cannot be wrathful is consonant with Paul's view of God's love for us.[18] More importantly, because sin caused both *our* wrath and anger toward self, others, and even God, she confessed that she would rather suffer all the pains of earth, death, purgatory, and hell than commit sin. Some contemporary commentators concur and insist that the content of wrath is purely human—God simply handing us over to ourselves.

However, I prefer to understand God's wrath metaphorically, as an anthropomorphic way of expressing what happens when holiness encounters evil. It refers to something that is in some sense both in God, in us, as

18. Julian of Norwich, *Showings*, chap. 46, 259; chap. 48, 262–63.

well as in the world. Wrath is what evil experiences in the presence of the Holy. In my view, wrath is the violence of God's *holy love* against whatever opposes or is contrary to the triune God's loving holiness. A pleasant God is a figment of the imagination of a shallow and cheerful Western liberalism. There is not a trace of a non-indignant God in the scriptures. The Epistle to the Hebrews proclaims that "it is a dreadful thing to fall into the hands of the living God" (Heb 10:31).

Thus, with the hope secured because of Jesus-Messiah's crucifixion, Paul stood back and surveyed the entire biblical narrative from Adam to Jesus-Messiah, who has inaugurated a new creation, not simply a return to the original creation. Here again is the goal of salvation—not to be saved for heaven, which Paul never mentions—but for the new creation. This restores the genuine human destiny: the covenant of vocation in which humans are called as a royal priesthood. This underscores that Paul is not concerned about escaping hell and going to heaven (more on this in a later chapter). Paul had in mind the covenant of vocation in which humans who find salvation in Jesus-Messiah become active participants, free from the lure and drag of the dark forces that had previously prevented this, within the work of new creation here and now. Thus, the cross is where the victorious Christ the King descended into hell, the realm of godlessness, and conquered SATAN, SIN, and DEATH in an apocalyptic battle that fully reveals the triumph of the trinitarian God's love for us. The Christian paradox: victory though defeat; resurrected life through a gruesome death.

In *The Vikings* TV series, the Viking chieftain Ragnar and his men failed twice to conquer Paris. To his men's disgust, Ragnar converted to Christianity—on condition that when he died, his obsequies and burial be in the cathedral, and that his men be allowed to be present at the city gates. With the king and the archbishop agreeing to these terms, Ragnar was baptized. Shortly thereafter, Ragnar died, was placed in a coffin, and brought into the Paris cathedral. As the coffin was set down, the fully armed and much alive Ragnar smashed out of the coffin, thrust his sword into the archbishop, and then held it to the king's throat. The city gates were opened and Paris fell to the Vikings. A brilliant ruse and one I see as somewhat analogous to Christ's death on the cross in terms of his descent into hell.

Paul's mysticism of the cross obliquely asserts that God's Word became flesh in order to invade the kingdom ruled by SATAN, SIN, and DEATH. Christ's ushered in God's kingdom and crushed Satan's kingdom. The paradox: the apocalyptic war between two kingdoms and two lords was waged by the sinless God-man who became sin and endured both the shame and curse of the cross. God became sin? God cursed God? Why? To use Satan's very weapons against Satan—on our behalf and for our sins. The early church fathers portrayed Christ as "the Deity . . . hidden under the veil of our nature, that so, as with ravenous fish, the hook of the Deity might be gulped down along with the bait of flesh, and thus, life being introduced into the house of death, and light shining in darkness, that which is diametrically opposed to light and life might vanish; for it is not in the nature of darkness to remain when light is present, or of death to exist when life is active."[19] The invading, plundering, binding, warrior Christ, in blazing white, strides triumphantly over the shattered gates of hell. Sheer majesty and dominion, the triumphant expedition of the victorious Christ the King is dramatized in many artistic works, known as the harrowing of hell.[20]

A Christian should view Christ's descent into hell through his death on the cross, as his cosmic conquest. In this way, he destroyed the power SATAN, SIN, and DEATH not only over people past, present, and future—the godly and the ungodly—but also the entire creation. As Paul wrote: "May I never boast except in the cross of our Lord Jesus Christ, through which the world has been crucified to me, and I to the world. Neither circumcision nor uncircumcision means anything; what counts is the new creation" (Gal 6:14–15). Paul's mysticism of the cross is the key to understanding his mysticism of the new creation, to be treated in a later chapter.

---

19. Gregory of Nyssa, *The Great Catechism*, chap. 24. Cited in Aulén, *Christus Victor*, 68.

20. A stunning example is the *Harrowing of Hades* fresco in the *parecclesion* of the Cora church in Istanbul c. 1315. The icon depicts Jesus, vested in white and gold to symbolize his divine majesty, standing on the brazen gates of Hades (also called the "Doors of Death"), which are broken and have fallen in the form of a cross, illustrating the belief that by his death on the cross, Jesus "trampled down death by death." He is holding Adam and Eve and pulling them up out of Hades. Traditionally, he is not shown holding them by the hands but by their wrists, to illustrate the theological teaching that humankind could not pull itself out of its original sin, but that it could come about only by God's work. Jesus is surrounded by various righteous figures from the Old Testament (Abraham, David, et al.). The bottom of the icon shows Hades as a chasm of darkness, often with various pieces of broken locks and chains strewn about. Quite frequently, one or two figures are shown in the darkness, bound in chains, who are generally identified as personifications of Death or Satan.

Paul's Mysticism of the Resurrection

"Have I not seen Jesus our Lord?" (1 Cor 9:1)

The bodily resurrection of Jesus-Messiah is the foundation of Christian faith and the event that sheds the most light on the dark mystery of existence. It is not simply one truth among the many other truths of the faith, but the absolute basis and reason for faith. Thus, one should believe *because* of the bodily resurrection. Why did the apostles come to believe? Why did they go out and preach at the risk of their own lives? Why were the Gospels and the rest of the New Testament penned? In light of what were they written?

Jesus' bodily resurrection became the light in which and the "eyeglasses" through which his ascension, crucifixion, passion, miracles, kingdom-centered preaching, childhood, infancy, and preexistence were viewed and understood by his apostles and the writers of the New Testament. If Jesus-Messiah had not been raised bodily from the dead, we would have never heard of him. And in a very short time, Jesus-Messiah was proclaimed as the name above all other names—even above Caesar's, which was political dynamite. The politically subversive aspect of the resurrection has not been sufficiently emphasized. In short, Christian faith is bodily resurrection faith, nothing less. As the apostle Paul wrote in 1 Corinthians 15:17–19: "And if Christ has not been raised, your faith is futile; you are still in your sins. . . . If only for this life we have hope in Christ, we are of all people most to be pitied."

Contrary to popular and even some scholarly opinion, *reason* grounds resurrection faith. First, it is reasonably certain that the tomb was empty because *women* witnessed it. Women were not legal witnesses and could not testify in court. If one is concocting a hoax, why depend upon those who are a priori excluded? Also, anti-Christian polemicists have never denied that the tomb was empty. The first conspiracy theory asserted that the body had been stolen (Matt 28:11–15). If, the tomb had not been empty, it would have been checked and Christianity could not have lasted one day. To paraphrase the statement of the renowned Swiss Reformed theologian Karl Barth (d. 1968), one must confess that although Christians do not believe in the empty tomb but in the living Jesus-Messiah, this does not imply that they can believe in the living Jesus-Messiah without believing in the empty tomb.

Second, grounded in an earlier tradition, Paul himself offered a powerful basis for the reasonableness of resurrection faith: a list of *credible* eyewitnesses who saw the risen Jesus-Messiah: Cephas, James, the Twelve, more than five hundred people at the same time, all the apostles, and then Paul himself (1 Cor 15:4–8). This testimony so shocked the German Lutheran theologian Rudolf Bultmann (d. 1976) and his followers that they called Paul's text "dangerous" because a list of credible eyewitnesses might compel a skeptic to believe in Jesus-Messiah. However, Paul did precisely that, which contradicts Bultmann's pure-faith view. Christian faith must be reasonable (1 Pet 3:15).

Paul and many contemporary scholars would have rightly rejected the views of recent and contemporary neo-gnostics, who contend that nothing happened to Jesus after his death but that the apostles finally came to see and accept the meaning of Jesus' life of self-sacrificing love.[21] Briefly put, Jesus rose into the hearts of his disciples and rose into the preaching of the early church.[22] Paradigmatic of such view is the German-born British biblical scholar Hubert J. Richards, who wrote:

> Yet seeing the risen Christ and believing in the resurrection are one and the same thing. The first is simply a more concrete way of expressing that faith. . . . Faith *is* the meeting with the risen Christ. . . . There is no other resurrection apart from the one which people experience today. Resurrection is not something different from the experience of Christ living on in us. . . . It is people, with their faith, who constitute the body of Christ. They *are* the risen Christ. There is no other.[23]

Paul's famous speech to the Athenians offers evidence of such an incorrect understanding of Jesus' bodily resurrection. Luke wrote:

> A group of Epicurean and Stoic philosophers began to debate with [Paul]. Some of them asked, "What is this babbler trying to say?" Others remarked, "He seems to be advocating foreign gods." They said this because Paul was preaching the good news about Jesus and the *resurrection*. . . . "In the past God overlooked such ignorance [about idols], but now he commands all people everywhere to repent. For he has set a day when he will judge the world with justice by the man he has appointed. He has given proof of this to everyone by *raising him from the dead*." When they heard about the *resurrection of the dead*, some of them

21. Wright, *The Resurrection*; O'Collins, *Believing in the Resurrection*.

22. Marxsen, *The Resurrection* esp. chs. 3–4; Winter, *The Trial*.

23. Richards, *The First Easter*, 59, 61, 69. His emphases.

sneered, but others said, "We want to hear you again on this subject." (Acts 17:18–32, my emphasis)

This text makes clear that although his debaters sneered and rejected Paul's teaching, they did understand what they were rejecting: nothing less than Paul's proclamation of Jesus' *bodily* resurrection. For both the Jews and gentiles of Paul's day, a non-bodily resurrection was an oxymoron. Resurrection was most definitely understood to mean *bodily* resurrection.

Many books that I read treated Jesus' bodily resurrection almost as an afterthought, if they treated it at all. They often explained it as God the Father patting Jesus on the back for a job well done, but not as the key element in Jesus' inauguration of the kingdom of God on earth as it is in heaven—the real meaning of the world's salvation. Did not St. Paul stress that he was called to be an apostle to preach the gospel of God concerning Jesus, designated Son of God according to the Holy Spirit by his bodily resurrection from the dead (Rom 1:1–5)? Paul likewise emphasized that Jesus was put to death for our sins and raised bodily for our justification (Rom 4:25). The Word became flesh and remains flesh for all eternity. More than one theologian has written profoundly of the eternal significance of Jesus' humanity.[24]

Three days after Jesus' crucifixion, his tomb was found empty. Then he appeared to his disciples in a "transformed physicality" (N. T. Wright) for which there was no expectation or precedent. This demonstrated to his first followers the truth of Jesus' pre-crucifixion claims that he really was Israel's Messiah. Paul's entire worldview remained solidly grounded in Judaism but a Judaism now dramatically rethought around Jesus and particularly around his resurrection. The controlling narratives included creation and exodus. The different aspects of Paul's apostolic practice—the gentile mission, prayer, apostolic suffering, his collection from gentile churches to help the impoverished Jewish ones—all grew out of a Jewish, indeed Pharisaical worldview, but had been turned inside out by the resurrection. It was only because Paul believed that God's new age had arrived that he judged that it was time for gentiles to hear the good news.

There is no pre-Christian evidence for a belief in a dying Messiah or the bodily resurrection of one person before the end of this age. Jesus' bodily resurrection—combined with the Jewish expectation of the end of the exile, Yhwh's return, and the presence of Jesus' Holy Spirit—generated a fresh reading of the messianic texts in the Jewish scriptures, which

24. Rahner, "Eternal Significance," 35–46.

enabled the disciples to grasp Jesus-Messiah's true identity. In the context of worship and awareness of the presence and power of the bodily risen Jesus-Messiah, biblical texts that had been there all along but never seen in this way sprang into new life. The earliest understanding of Jesus' identity was thus firmly anchored in the Jewish scriptures. However, this reading of scripture was highly innovative and did not itself generate belief in Jesus-Messiah. The empty tomb and Jesus' appearances were necessary. Did not Jesus himself give the Emmaus disciples a lesson in scripture, as found in Luke 24:27: "And beginning with Moses and all the Prophets, he explained to them what was said in all the scriptures concerning himself"? This points to the earliest example of the meaning of the word *mystical*: discovering how the Jewish scriptures refer to Jesus—and one of the definitions of *mystical* used in this book.

Early Christianity, with reference to bodily resurrection, looked much like a variety of Pharisaic Judaism and was connected with the return from exile. However, it is somewhat anomalous that in Second Temple Judaism resurrection was a somewhat peripheral belief. However, early Christianity made Jesus-Messiah's bodily resurrection central and so did Paul. Judaism was almost always quite vague as to what sort of a body the resurrected person would possess. Yet right from the start, early Christianity focused on a new body of transformed physicality, in the sense of a physical object occupying space and time.

Scholars use the term collaborative eschatology to stress Paul's belief that the resurrection had begun with Jesus and would be completed in the great final bodily resurrection of all on the Last Day. He believed that God had called him and his followers to work with him through the power of the Holy Spirit to put into practice what Jesus-Messiah required. This would anticipate the final resurrection, through holiness in personal and political life. It was not merely that God had inaugurated the end. Paul understood Jesus-Messiah's bodily resurrection as the arrival now of God's future. Jesus' followers were charged with and empowered by his Holy Spirit to transform the present, as far as they were able, in the light of that future. Paul also wrote of resurrection as referring metaphorically to baptism, which he viewed as a symbolic (in contemporary terms, a sacramental) dying with and a rising with Christ. It also underscored the new life of strenuous ethical obedience, enabled by the Holy Spirit. These metaphorical meanings are regularly found right alongside passages in which the literal meaning of a future actual bodily resurrection is also emphasized. Once more, all these meanings make sense only when understood in the Jewish world of thought.

A dying and risen Messiah made no initial sense in a Jewish context. Where messianic speculations existed, the Messiah was supposed to fight God's victorious battle against the wicked pagans, rebuild the temple, and bring God's justice into the world. Jesus had done none of these things. Moreover, he died ignominiously at the hands of the pagans rather than defeating them in battle. But from early on, Christians, and emphatically Paul, affirmed that Jesus was indeed the Messiah, precisely because of the resurrection. Thus, it is impossible to account for the early Christian belief in Jesus as Messiah without the resurrection. The very early Christians and certainly Paul proclaimed the belief that the risen Jesus is Lord and therefore Caesar is not. Already in Paul, the resurrection—both of Jesus and then in the future of his people—is the foundation of the Christian stance of allegiance to a different King, a different Lord. Also, Lord Death-Sin-Satan had been defeated.

It bears emphasizing that those who believed in the bodily resurrection were burned at the stake and thrown to the lions. However, it was the gnostics who hated the body (though how they enjoyed using it!), denied bodily resurrection, and used resurrection language to describe subjective, interior spirituality. They escaped persecution. The Christian proclamation of bodily resurrection was always bound to get one into trouble and it regularly did. So much for the nonsense that Christianity has nothing to do with politics and the social order.

Paul wrote in a classic passage, Romans 8:23: "we know that the whole creation has been groaning in travail together until now; and not only the creation, but we ourselves, who have the first fruits of the Spirit, groan inwardly as we wait for adoption as sons, the redemption of our bodies." God's people were promised a new type of bodily existence, the fulfillment and redemption of our present bodily life. When Paul wrote in Philippians 3:20 of being citizens of heaven, he did not mean that we shall retire there when we have finished our work here. He declared that Jesus will come *from heaven* in order to transform the present humble body into a glorious body like his own. For Paul, the risen Jesus-Messiah is both a model for the Christian's future body and the means by which it will come about.

Likewise, Paul declared in Colossians 3:4 that when the Messiah appears, then we too will appear with him in glory. Paul does not say that one day we will go to be with him in heaven. No, we already possess life in him. This new life, which the Christian possesses secretly, invisible to the world, will burst forth into full bodily reality and visibility—the new creation, thy kingdom come *on earth* as it is in heaven. The clearest and strongest passage about bodily resurrection, yet often ignored, is Romans 8:11: "And if the Spirit of him who raised Jesus from the dead is living in you, he who raised Christ from the dead will also give life to your mortal bodies because of his Spirit who lives in you." Thus, Paul affirmed that God will give us life, not as disembodied spirits, not as what many people think of as a spiritual body in the sense of a nonphysical one, but as transformed physical body-persons. Resurrection is therefore a way of speaking about a new bodily life after whatever state of existence one might enter immediately upon death. In other words bodily resurrection means, in the words of N. T. Wright, "life after life after death."

In writing about his apostleship in 2 Corinthians 4:14, Paul proclaimed that "we know that the one who raised the Lord Jesus from the dead will also raise us with Jesus and present us with you to himself." Thus, the God who raised Jesus from the dead will also raise us up with Jesus to bring us into his presence. He also stressed how God's power showed itself in him as an "earthen vessel" with his outer nature wasting away but his inner nature being renewed daily (2 Cor 4:7). This text goes on to announce the "eternal house," "new tent," "tabernacle," and "new body" waiting within God's sphere—again heaven—ready to put on over the present body so that what is mortal may be become immortal. As Paul wrote:

> For we know that if the earthly tent we live in is destroyed, we have a building from God, an eternal house in heaven, not built by human hands. . . . Now the one who has fashioned us for this very purpose is God, who has given us the Spirit as a deposit, guaranteeing what is to come. . . . We are confident, I say, and would prefer to be away from the body and at home with the Lord. So we make it our goal to please him, whether we are at home in the body or away from it. For we must all appear before the judgment seat of Christ, so that each of us may receive what is due us for the things done while in the body, whether good or bad. (2 Cor 5:1–10)

As was his wont, Paul insisted that God will accomplish this by the Holy Spirit. His point here is not that bodies die and decay and that the only way to be permanent, unchanging, and immortal is to become nonphysical. Rather, he accentuated a new kind of physicality (transformed physicality, in the words of N. T. Wright) that stands in relation to our present body—as Jesus' transformed, risen body does to his pre-resurrection body. It will be much more real, more bodily than our present body as our present body is more substantial, more touchable, than a disembodied spirit. We sometimes speak of someone who has been very ill as being a shadow of his or her former self. Thus, in Paul's view, a Christian in this present life is a mere shadow of his or her future self, the self that person will be when the body that God has waiting in his heavenly storeroom is brought out, already made-to-measure, and put on over the present one— or over the self that will still exist after bodily death. In this text, he also focused on our appearance before the judgment seat of the Messiah, and for that we shall need bodies.

Contradicting those who deny bodily resurrection, Paul's chapter 15 of his First Letter to the Corinthians highlights that Jesus-Messiah is the first fruits of the great harvest still to come when all his people are raised as he was. The entire chapter alludes to the book of Genesis and is a theology of the new creation. It focuses on two types of bodies, the present one and the future one. The popular translation of key phrases, such as *physical* body and *spiritual* body, distorts Paul's contrast between the corruptible, decaying, and doomed-to-die present body, and the incorruptible, never-to-die-again future body. The issue does not center on a physical and a Platonic or gnostic nonphysical body but on the power or energy that animates the body. A ship may be wind or nuclear powered. The present body, which is animated by the normal human life-force, is ultimately powerless against illness, injury, decay, and death. God's Holy Spirit, the energizing power of God's new creation, will animate the future body. One might say this present body, planted as a physical acorn, will be raised as a might oak animated by the Holy Spirit.

Jesus' bodily resurrection through the Holy Spirit had *sublated* his original earthly person. Sublation means that what sublates goes beyond what is sublated (the pre-Easter Jesus), introduces something new and distinct, and puts everything on a new basis. But so far from interfering with the sublated or destroying it, on the contrary it needs it, includes it, preserves all its proper features and properties, and carries them forward to a fuller realization within a richer context (the risen Jesus-Messiah with transformed physicality).

For example, if Quantum physics goes beyond and carries forward the proper features and properties of Newtonian physics to a superior realization within a richer context, then Jesus' *new creation* physics does the same to both Quantum and Newtonian physics. Contrary to the Enlightenment's naive view of miracles, they violate the laws of nature only as they are now understood. The far better view depends upon the theology Duns Scotus, who maintained that God created in order to communicate Godself and that creation itself exists in order to be the recipient of God's free gift of self. Because creation is open to God's self-communication, the incarnation and Jesus' resurrection are indications that miracles are a compelling sign that the risen Christ is creation's goal, the seed of the new creation, who will transform and perfect all creation.

It bears repeating that Paul contrasted not what we call physical and what we call nonphysical but *corruptible physicality* on the one hand and with *incorruptible physicality* on the other. This underlies the salient conclusion of 1 Corinthians 15:

> For the trumpet will sound, the dead will be raised imperishable, and we will be changed. For the perishable must clothe itself with the imperishable, and the mortal with immortality. When the perishable has been clothed with the imperishable, and the mortal with immortality, then the saying that is written will come true: "Death has been swallowed up in victory." "Where, O death, is your victory? Where, O death, is your sting?" The sting of death is sin, and the power of sin is the law. But thanks be to God! He gives us the victory through our Lord Jesus Christ. Therefore, my dear brothers and sisters, stand firm. Let nothing move you. Always give yourselves fully to the work of the Lord, because you know that your labor in the Lord is not in vain.

The resurrection means that what we do in the present, and the toil we do for the gospel, is not wasted. As Maximus said, in the excellent film *Gladiator*, what we do here resounds for all eternity—in ways at which we can only guess.

This is the proper context for understanding what Paul wrote concerning his sufferings: "Therefore we do not lose heart. Though outwardly we are wasting away, yet inwardly we are being renewed day by day. For our light and momentary troubles are achieving for us an eternal glory that far outweighs them all. So we fix our eyes not on what is seen, but on what is unseen, since what is seen is temporary, but what is unseen is eternal" (2 Cor 4:16–18). Paul likewise emphasized that just as the wounds of the risen Christ were not sources of pain and death, but glorious and signs of his victory, so the Christian's risen body will bear such marks of his or her loyalty to God's particular calling as are appropriate, not least where this has involved suffering.

Therefore, Jesus-Messiah's disciples were looking at the first—and so far, the only—occurrence of incorruptible physicality. The risen Christ was the transformed yet same pre-risen Jesus. Of course, there may well be some bodily continuity between this body and our future one, as was Jesus himself, but God is well capable of re-creating people even if—as with the martyrs of Lyons—their ashes are scattered into a fast flowing river. Is not even our present body a mystery? Consider that the one body-person develops from the zygote, the developing unborn child, baby, young child, teenager, young person, middle aged and old aged person, then a very old person just before death, which discloses a mysterious *identity in transformation* even this side of death. If God created out of nothing, then when the question of how the dead are raised comes up, the answer is always, by the Holy Spirit. The same Spirit who brooded over the waters of chaos indwells Jesus so richly that he is known as the Spirit of Jesus. The Holy Spirit, already present within Jesus' followers as the first-fruits, is the down payment, the guarantee of what is to come. The Holy Spirit is the Lord and Giver of life. In Paul's powerful words: "If you declare with your mouth, 'Jesus is Lord,' and believe in your heart that God raised him from the dead, you will be saved" (Rom 10:9).

Chapter 4

A Trinitarian *Shema* Mysticism

"There are different kinds of gifts, but the same Spirit distributes them. There are different kinds of service, but the same Lord. There are different kinds of working, but in all of them and in everyone it is the same God at work" (1 Cor 12:4–6)

A Mysticism of the Father

"Because you are his sons, God sent the Spirit of his Son into our hearts, the Spirit who calls out, 'Abba, Father.'" (Gal 4:6)

YEARS AGO, A JESUIT friend, working on his doctoral dissertation in scripture, told me that there was no Trinity in the Bible. I replied that I had been baptized in the name (notice: singular, one God) of the Father, the Son, and the Holy Spirit. Moreover, Arthur W. Wainwright's 1962 classic, *The Trinity in the New Testament*, definitively proved the Jesuit's view false. More to the point, so many Pauline scholars in recent years have focused on the Trinity that one can speak of a nascent school of trinitarian interpreters—thus a trinitarian renaissance.[1]

Of course, one does not find in the New Testament the metaphysical Trinity of the later tradition, with its technical terms, such as "person," "hypostasis," "perichoresis, "circumincession," and the like. However, I agree with those scholars who affirm that a proto- or incipient Trinity is deeply rooted in the New Testament. For example, Paul emphasized the irreducible threeness of the uniquely one God's identity shown through God's activity in and among his people. I maintain that Paul viewed God not simply as God, but as the Father of our Lord Jesus Christ and the one

1. Hill, *Paul and the Trinity*, esp. 36–43, 167–72.

who raised Jesus from the dead through the power of the Holy Spirit.[2] Thus, I find in Paul a trinitarian *Shema* mysticism and do not share the view of Albert Schweitzer, who reduced Paul's mysticism to only a "being-in-Christ" mysticism.

As a zealous, blameless Pharisee, Saul would have had an exceptionally profound *Shema* spirituality. To the young Saul of Tarsus, believing in one God of Israel meant family, flesh, blood, breath, prayer, persecution, life itself—not philosophical speculation. What is more, Paul knew a highly practical meaning of monotheism: allegiance to the one God meant persecution from the surrounding world—sometimes from his fellow Jews.

For example, the great Rabbi Akiba, arrested for continuing to teach the Torah in defiance of the Roman edict and for his support of the Simon bar Kokhbar rebellion, was asked by one of the Roman torturers as they were slowly killing him why he was reciting the *Shema*. He said that up until now he had been able to love the LORD with all his might and heart, but at this moment, the time had come to love him with his very life. He then continued to recite the prayer, *the LORD is one,* until he died. This is what monotheism meant for Second Temple Judaism.

So, for Saul of Tarsus, monotheism was the pellucid and unflinching belief that Israel's God was the Creator of all, the *only* God. Monotheism likewise focused on the God of the exodus, a God who would return in person to rescue his people and dwell in their midst. Moreover, Israel's God was the real King—a politically explosive stance, given the times. Monotheism and the kingdom of God were firmly linked. Move over Caesar!

The zealous monotheism of the Second Temple period came to expression not least in the context of extreme *suffering*. Israel's God alone is worthy of the name God. He will rescue Israel, if not from suffering and death, then through it at the final bodily resurrection. He will also eventually judge those who worship idols and have behaved with arrogance, folly, and cruelty. Jewish monotheists understood evil not to be inherent in creation but as the result of idolatry and looked for the day when Israel's God would set up his kingdom of justice and peace. Monotheism, election, eschatology all go together. Monotheism therefore meant the

2. McGrath, *The Only True God*, 40, is paradigmatic of those who contend that Paul had expanded rather than split the *Shema*. In his view, God and Jesus together do *not* constitute one God. Rather, there is one God and there is one Lord—both alongside one another, and yet the second one occupying a subordinate, mediator role in relation to the first. An example of those who maintain that Paul reconceived Jewish monotheism as a *trinitarian* monotheism, see Dunn, *The Cambridge Companion to St. Paul*, 264–65.

renunciation of ontological dualism, that is, renouncing the world itself, pretending it was an evil place, or deeply disturbed about the soul being imprisoned within a material body—as later Gnosticism would claim. The one God had created everything good. Thus, Paul affirmed the goodness in the God-givenness of the created world, of human beings as image of this good God, of the goodness of food and drink, of marriage, of sexuality, and even of political structures. The one God will judge an out-of-joint world and in so doing will put the world right, in line with his promises. This is the monotheism in and through which Saul came to believe that the one God is Father, Son, and Holy Spirit.

Paul's gospel, as stated in Romans 1:1–6, bears repeating:

> Paul, a servant of Christ Jesus, called to be an apostle and set apart for the gospel of God—the gospel he promised beforehand through his prophets in the Holy Scriptures regarding his Son, who as to his earthly life was a descendant of David, and who through the Spirit of holiness was appointed the Son of God in power by his resurrection from the dead: Jesus Christ our Lord. Through him we received grace and apostleship to call all the Gentiles to the obedience that comes from faith for his name's sake. And you also are among those Gentiles who are called to belong to Jesus Christ.

Evidence shows that although Paul regarded God as one, he identified this one and only God as the Father of our Lord Jesus Christ. Although the title *God* was occasionally given to Christ, the title *Father* never was. The title *Lord*, which was given to God in the Old Testament, is used in the New Testament both of God the Father and Jesus-Messiah the Son. The functions of judgment, creation, and salvation are ascribed to both Father and Son. It would have been fitting for an anointed king to be called the father of his people. But in fact the title *Father* was limited only to the Father of Jesus Christ.

The Christian belief in the Fatherhood of God has its roots in the Jewish tradition. Although *Father* is not a common title for God in the First Testament, it does proclaim the Creator God as Father to Israel in the sense that the Creator God adopted Israel, with the covenant as the formal ceremony of adoption. The people are his sons, with the nation collectively as his son. God was also described as the Father of the anointed king. The description of God as the Father of the whole world can be found, but it remains exceptional. God's Fatherhood is usually explained by his protective care for the Jewish people.

No Gospel proclaims God as the Father of both Jesus himself and the disciples *together*. God is *either* Jesus' Father or the disciples' Father. The absolute Father in Mark 13:32—only the Father knows when the end of this age will come—is so closely linked with the Son that it is clear that in this verse *God* refers to *Jesus'* Father. When Jesus used the word *Abba* of God, he was stressing a relationship with God that was closer than any of his countrymen could claim. Paul also emphasized the fatherhood of God and often used the phrase *the God and Father of our Lord Jesus Christ*. On occasion he does designate God as our Father. Although Paul often regarded God as the Father of Jesus-Messiah and of Christian believers, in Ephesians 4:6 he is described as the "one God and Father of all, who is over all and through all and in all." The distinctive emphasis upon God's *Fatherhood of Jesus-Messiah* enabled Christians to conceive of a Father-Son relationship within the Godhead and to discover a *plurality* within the unity of the Godhead.

Paul's astonishing Damascus-road encounter with the risen Christ engendered in him a mystically transformed *Shema* so that the one God would be understood to include his Son and the Holy Spirit so that Paul would later proclaim: "Because you are his sons, God sent the Spirit of his Son into our hearts, the Spirit who calls out, 'Abba, Father'" (Gal 4:6). Just as Jesus called God his *Abba*, beloved Father, and taught his disciples to do the same, Paul also employed this strikingly intimate form of address to God—which no Jew would have used. Jesus said explicitly: "And do not call anyone on earth 'father,' for you have one Father, and he is in heaven" (Matt 23:9).

The bidirectionality (a tridirectionality will be discussed later) of Paul's mysticism caused him to identify Jesus not only in relation to God but also *to identify God in relation to Jesus*. Only in relation to the *Father* is Jesus the *Son*. Likewise, the Father is only who he is in relation to Jesus the Son. Thus, the apostle Paul interpreted God's *identity* and action by way of Jesus-Messiah. Thus, Paul's God and Father language interacts and is intertwined with his Jesus-Messiah language. One finds sprinkled throughout Paul's epistles the proclamation that God the *Father* raised Jesus from the dead. For example, Paul came to describe God as "the one who raised Jesus our Lord from the dead, the one who justifies the ungodly, and the one who gives life to the dead" (Rom 4:24–25). Because of Paul's conviction that God raised the crucified Jesus-Messiah to a new and transformed life—this is not resuscitation—he reread the Genesis narrative in a new light. For instance, because Abraham's body and Sarah's womb were as good as dead—but Sarah became pregnant—Paul stressed God's identity as the giver of life *because of Jesus' bodily resurrection from the dead*. Paul wrote of the Abraham event another way: "The promises were spoken to Abraham and to his seed. Scripture does not say 'and to seeds,' meaning many people, but 'and to your seed,' meaning one person, who is Christ" (Gal 3:16). It would be difficult to overemphasize how important the single-family-in-Christ theme was for Paul.

A traditional Judeo-Christian teaching believed that the very act of biblical exegesis could be *mystically* transformative. Yes, but one can also argue that the reverse can also be true. Pau's mystical encounter with the risen Christ on the Damascus road and his later revelations enabled him to read the Jewish scriptures in the light of the risen Jesus-Messiah. Paul creatively linked Sarah's dead womb, which became pregnant with Isaac, *and* the justification of the ungodly to the event of God raising Jesus from the dead. Therefore, according to Paul's way of thinking, the God of Abraham always was the God who raised Jesus-Messiah from the dead, even prior to the actual event. This means that Abraham's God was and is the God who would raise Jesus bodily from the dead. In short, in Paul's view, God's very identity as the God of Abraham must have involved reference to the risen Jesus-Messiah.

One finds another correlation in Paul: "You, however, are not in the realm of the flesh but are in the realm of the Spirit, if indeed the Spirit of God lives in you. And if anyone does not have the Spirit of Christ, they do not belong to Christ. But if Christ is in you, then even though your body is subject to death because of sin, the Spirit gives life because of righteousness. And if the Spirit of him who raised Jesus from the dead is living in you, he who raised Christ from the dead will also give life to your mortal bodies because of his Spirit who lives in you" (Rom 8:9–11). Although this text contains a tridirectionality, the role of the Holy Spirit will be taken up only later. The emphasis here is now only on the bidirectionality or mutuality of God and the risen Jesus-Messiah. Paul's chapter moves on to state that *God did not spare his own Son* (Rom 8:32), which connects with the God who raised Jesus from the dead. If *God* is identified by his act of raising Jesus, then he is equally *identified* by his giving up Jesus as *his Son* whom he sent for that purpose. This Christological divine action determined Paul's understanding of God's purpose as it was *prior* to the Jesus-Messiah event. God's foreknowledge and predestination of the believers to whom Paul wrote is probably best understood as the witness to the inclusion of gentiles into God's one family that he understood from the Jewish scriptures.

Obviously, to discern a Jesus-Messiah oriented identity of God prior to the Christ event underscores that in Paul's view God does not become what God was not. Paul did not know a time when God was not already the God who would send his Son so that believers might be conformed to his image. Thus, God cannot be *identified* as God apart from the Jesus-Messiah event. To Paul's way of thinking, even before the sending of the Son, God's very identity was bound up with the Son. It is astonishing that some scholars deny this.

Paul's Letter to the Galatians also focuses on the primal mark of God's identity: "Paul, an apostle—sent not from men nor by a man, but by Jesus Christ and God the Father, who raised him from the dead" (Gal 1:1). By putting side by side God's act of bodily raising Jesus from the dead with the title *Father*, Paul brings out not only the Father-Son relationship but also the relationship between the sonship of Jesus and the sonship of the Galatians themselves. This epistle likewise refers to Abraham: "If you belong to Christ, then you are Abraham's seed, and heirs according to the promise" (Gal 3:29). Thus, also here, Paul identified God as the one who raised Jesus from the dead, which illuminates God's act of giving life to Abraham's body and Sarah's womb. The accompanying name *Father* is part of an argument that urges Paul's hearers to look to Abraham as their father in sharing his faith in a particular way apart from circumcision. This is another instance of Paul emphasizing that Jesus-Messiah is intrinsic to a true understanding of monotheism. He insisted that God's calling of Abraham was inseparable from its later historical revelation of the crucified and risen Jesus-Messiah and the Son of God the Father.

I wish to emphasize—in agreement with many contemporary scholars—that the identities of the persons of the Trinity are determined by means of their relation with and to each other. This chapter aims to highlight the bidirectionality of the Father who raised Jesus from the dead and Jesus-Messiah as the Son of this Father. If asked what makes God the God who justifies the ungodly, the answer is the God who raised Jesus from the dead. If asked about what designates the God who gave life to Sarah's dead womb, again the answer is the God who raised Jesus from the dead. If asked what makes God the God who predestines and foreknows people and adopts them in fulfillment of promises made to Abraham, the answer is the same: the God who raised Jesus from the dead. In other words, God was always known by Paul in reference to his Son, Jesus Christ.

The central point is *not* exactly what others have described as the inclusion of Jesus within the identity of God in such a way that monotheism is expanded so that it might include Jesus' action and identity. Rather, what is salient is Paul's claim that the action of God's raising Jesus-Messiah bodily from the dead became not only the occasion of *identifying* God but also made possible a grasp of *God's very identity*—what makes God the unique person God is vis-à-vis Jesus Christ, that is, God the Father. Consequently, what identifies God as the God who gave life to Sarah's dead womb, the God who predestined and foreknew a people and adopted them in fulfillment of promises made to Abraham, is the God whose *aim* had always involved God's Son, Jesus Christ, whom the Father raised from the dead. In other words, the one God, mystically known and loved, is always the God of Jesus Christ.

A Mysticism of the Son

"There is but one Lord, Jesus Christ, through whom all things came and through whom we live." (1 Cor 8:6)

Paul knew that he had dramatically reinterpreted monotheism around Jesus himself, a human being who lived, died, and rose in Paul's very recent memory. On the other hand, he did not add Jesus as a new God to a pantheon. Paul understood Jesus-Messiah as the human being in whom Israel's one and only God acted in Israel's history to do for Israel, humanity, and the world what they could not do for themselves. Thus, he comprehended Jesus as an essential aspect of the identity of Israel's God, and YHWH as intrinsic to Jesus' identity. In addition, Paul emphasized that the identities of YHWH and Jesus (and the Holy Spirit) are mutually constituted by one another—but in an asymmetrical fashion. God the Father is only so in relation to Jesus as his Son. Insofar as God is the Father who sent and raised his Son, his identity is constituted by that relationship to the Son. Thus, Paul wrote of the full inter-dependence of God the Father and Jesus-Messiah on each another for their distinct identities but not their interchangeability. Mutuality, yes, but not symmetry.

Thus, I agree with those scholars who reject the Enlightenment's reduction of Jesus to a great teacher whose followers—several decades later—tried to divinize him. I likewise deny the claim that Paul understood Jesus as playing only a subordinate, mediating role to YHWH.[3] The New Testament evidence shows that Jesus was not added to the one God as an especially honored agent but rather included within the unique divine identity as inseparable from God. Did not Paul write: "The Son is the image of the invisible God, the firstborn over all creation. For in him all things were created: things in heaven and on earth, visible and invisible, whether thrones or powers or rulers or authorities; all things have been created through him and for him. He is before all things, and in him all things hold together" (Col 1:15–17)? And then in 1 Corinthian 8:6: "yet for us there is one God, the Father, from whom are all things and for whom we exist, and one Lord, Jesus Christ, through whom are all things and through whom we exist"? And to drive home Paul's point: "For God was pleased to have all his fullness dwell in him, and through him to reconcile to himself all things, whether things on earth or things in heaven, by making peace through his blood, shed on the cross" (Col 1:19–20).

These texts indicate that Jesus' followers worshipped him in part because he had uniquely participated in the creation of all things. Moreover, some scholars translate the following texts this way: Romans 9:5: "of their Israelite race is the Christ according to the flesh, God who is over all" and Titus 2:3: "the glory of the great God and savior Jesus Christ." Thus, Paul does directly predicate the title God of Jesus.[4] Paul also frequently used the title *Lord* for Jesus, a clear reference to the Septuagint's translation of the Hebrew word for God. Especially salient is how early even Jewish Christians began to worship Jesus as God. Arians were later to contend that Jesus was only the highest creature and that there was "a time when he was not." The orthodox Christians retorted: "Then, why do you worship a creature?" The devotion given to Jesus was without a true analogy, and so is a remarkable and puzzling historical phenomenon.

In the past, scholars tended to focus on the titles predicated of Jesus but overlooked *devotional* practices.[5] For example, the significance of the practice of singing hymns about Jesus as God's Son were part of early Christian worship, thus worship of Jesus. So was prayer to God *through* Jesus and *in* Jesus' name and even direct prayer to Jesus himself, including particularly the invocation of Jesus in a corporate worship setting. Jesus'

---

3. Hurtado, *Lord Jesus Christ*; Bauckham, *God Crucified*.

4. Brown, "Does the New Testament Call Jesus God," 545–73.

5. Hurtado, *Lord Jesus Christ*.

name was invoked expressly in Christian baptism, healings, and exorcisms. The Christian common meal was understood as a sacred meal where the risen Jesus presides as *Lord*—the Old Testament name for God, *Adonai*, as found in the Septuagint—of the gathered community. Christian prophecy was realized as oracles of the risen Jesus-Messiah, and the Holy Spirit of prophecy was considered to be *Jesus'* Spirit.

This deep sense and experience of the personal presence of the exalted Jesus, in the way that one might expect to experience the presence of the living God, led Jesus' earliest disciples first to worship him—without any sense of compromising their monotheism—then to reread Israel's scriptures in such a way as to discover him in passages that were about the one God. It was the early Christian experience of the risen Lord in their midst in worship and prayer that formed the context within which *pre*-Christian Jewish ideas—such as the quasi-divine patriarchs, exalted angels, wisdom, and possibly even a messiah—come together and formed a new pattern in Paul's letters that Jesus was much more than merely human. These are some of the Jewish categories that the pre-Christian Saul would have had in mind and that were reconfigured by his Damascus-road encounter with Jesus risen.

This also accounts for the immense Jewish opposition to Jesus-Messiah devotion even prior to the destruction of Jerusalem in 70 A.D. From the earliest days of Jewish Christianity, it appears that devotion to Jesus was a cause of serious controversy and even oppression by some Jews, whether within their families or the larger Jewish community, who viewed Jesus devotion as a blasphemous threat to the uniqueness of Israel's one God. The zealous Pharisee Saul undoubtedly persecuted Jesus' followers with such ferocity because of their worship of the Jewish man Jesus, whom the Romans had crucified. In addition, the pagans despised Jesus' followers as atheists because they would not worship the Roman gods, but only a crucified messianic pretender whom they superstitiously claimed was bodily raised from the dead, and thus they disrupted the social order.

Paul's took monotheistic Old Testament passages that uniquely referred to Yhwh and applied them to the Lord Jesus Christ. This unambiguously indicates that he was convinced that Jesus and Yhwh mutually constituted each another's identities—without impairing their personal uniqueness. For instance, when Paul wrote that "everyone who calls upon the name of the Lord [i.e., Jesus] will be saved" (Rom 10:13), he was aware of the prophet Joel's utterance about God: "and it shall come to pass that all who call upon the name of the LORD shall be delivered" (Joel 2:32).

Perhaps Paul's most powerful example of using Jewish scriptures to transform Jewish monotheism is found in Isaiah 45:21–26. This supremely monotheistic text scathingly denounced the Babylonian gods for even attempting to steal the praise that is YHWH's alone. The text proclaims: "And there is no God apart from me, a righteous God and a Savior; there is none but me. Turn to me and be saved, all you ends of the earth; for I am God, and there is no other. By myself I have sworn, my mouth has uttered in all integrity a word that will not be revoked: Before me every knee will bend; by me every tongue will swear."

Consonant with Isaiah's text is the Christ hymn in Philippians, one of Paul's most beautiful texts and one of my favorites:

> In your relationships with one another, have the same mind as Christ Jesus: Who, being in very nature God, did not consider equality with God something to be used to his own advantage; rather, he made himself nothing by taking the very nature of a servant, being made in human likeness. And being found in appearance as a man, he humbled himself by becoming obedient to death—even death on a cross! Therefore God exalted him to the highest place and gave him the name that is above every name, that at the name of Jesus every knee should bend, in heaven and on earth and under the earth, and every tongue acknowledge that Jesus Christ is Lord, to the glory of God the Father. (Phil 2:5–11)

This is a clear link to the text, Isaiah 45:21–26.

Paul's important text revised Israel's monotheism of divine identity in the light of Jesus to underscore what it would look like when YHWH returned to Zion. YHWH had refused to share his glory with another. Now he shares it because Jesus-Messiah has accomplished the task that Israel's God had declared he himself would himself accomplish when he returned. The Philippians text also has echoes of Isaiah's humble, obedient suffering servant. Isaiah's text stressed as well the absolute uniqueness of Israel's God in his victory over all idols. Thus, "at the name of Jesus every knee shall bend and every tongue confess," replaces what YHWH said in reference to himself. But what Jesus' followers would now confess is not simply God, as in Isaiah, but that Jesus-Messiah is Lord. Again, when Paul writes *Lord* (*Kyrios*) in relation to Jesus, he uses the Greek word substituted for the divine name YHWH as found in the Septuagint.

Again, Paul did not add Jesus as a new God to a pantheon. He is the human being in whom YHWH, Israel's one and only God, has acted within cosmic history, and Israel's history to do for Israel, humanity, and the world what they could not do for themselves. Jesus was to be seen as part of the identity of Israel's God, and vice versa. When Paul proclaimed that Jesus had received the name that is over all names, that name is the holy divine name of YHWH. Jesus-Messiah is *Lord*, is *YHWH*—the name of the one true God over against all the other names that might be named around the world. Moreover, confessing Jesus as *Lord* brings glory to *God the Father*, just as one finds proclaimed in 1 Corinthians 15:26: "all things are put in subjection under the Messiah's feet, then the Messiah himself hands over the sovereignty to the Father, so that God is all in all." Thus, the unity and difference between Jesus the Lord and the Father. Paul also referred to Jesus as the human being who prior to his conception and birth—an implicit way of speaking of Jesus' preexistence?—was in God's form. Although equal with God, he neither cleaved to such a status nor abandoned it, but rather gave it its proper interpretation: a life of self-emptying, humble service that ended in death on a cross.

This text echoes what one finds in Genesis concerning Adam who was created to be God's vicegerent over all creation. However, he sought equality with God and incurred death. Jesus embraced the cross and for this reason is exalted. When Paul urged the Philippians to have the mind of Christ, this required a forceful monotheism fully rethought around Jesus-Messiah. This Messiah-shape monotheism, focused on the self-emptying and crucified Jesus, is the only thing that would enable the community to hold onto its unity and holiness—a key point in Paul's view of the one church (to be discussed in a later chapter). The Messiah's shameful crucifixion is the paradoxical but oddly appropriate focal point, the moment when the divine purpose was finally unveiled. At the center of the Philippians poem stands the sign of shame and glory. The entire scriptural vision of Israel's one God working out his sovereign purpose takes on here a radically new note. The obedient, suffering, crucified one—who, as one who hangs upon a tree, is cursed—is glorified and identified as Israel's God himself in person, which includes the promise that Israel's God would come back in person to rescue his people and establish the kingdom. Paul's picture of Jesus the Messiah exalted as Lord does not destroy Jewish monotheism. It fulfills it. For in Jesus-Messiah the fullness of divinity dwells bodily.

Be that as it may, to emphasize Jesus' divinity in this way ignores the Christian question of *how* this relates to the coming of God's kingdom *on earth* as it is in heaven, which is the gospel's central message and an essential theme for Paul as well. As a result, it is impossible to give an orthodox answer to the question "Is Jesus divine?" and to the subquestion, "When did the early Christians realize this?" while ignoring the dynamics of what Jesus, the embodied God, was actually doing. Second Temple monotheism believed that Israel's God had deserted Jerusalem and the temple during the Babylonian exile but would return one day—in person, in glory, as King, to destroy Israel's enemies and to usher in a new exodus.

What the pre-Christian Jews believed about God's future act of returning to Zion centered on what they believed about his actual identity. What YHWH *does* connects with who he actually *is*. Paul, with remarkable mystical genius, understood that Israel's God had done in Jesus what he had long promised to do. God had returned to be King and had inaugurated his kingdom *on earth* as it is in heaven. YHWH achieved the new exodus through Jesus' life, death, and bodily resurrection. Paul understood the messianic meaning of the sending of the Son as the mode of divine return. Thus, Paul also corrected the already dominant understanding of the story of Abraham and Isaac, elevating it in favor of the larger biblical story of Israel's God sending the servant or sending Wisdom to accomplish his divine purpose. This is implicit in the Galatians text: "Because you are his sons, God sent the Spirit of his Son into our hearts, the Spirit who calls out, 'Abba, Father'" (Gal 4:6).

Some Second Temple Jews, and then many early Christians, spoke of the strange and unexpected return of Israel's God as the Wisdom figure in the Jewish scriptures indicate. Second Temple belief in eschatological monotheism—the start of the new age—was at the heart of the divine identity, which included the themes of exodus, redemption, tabernacle, presence, return, Wisdom, and kingship. Only against this horizon can we understand how the first Christians came to understand Jesus in the way they did. And these themes definitely dominated Paul's consciousness.

Recent scholarship has definitively shown to be false a widely held earlier view that belief in Jesus' divinity arose only *after* the early Christians had lost their grip on their Jewish heritage.[6] Especially bogus, too, is the opinion that Jesus worship was derived from Caesar worship. Thus, some scholars wrongly held the opinion that the divinization of Jesus accidentally

---

6. See notes 3 and 4.

colluded with the long-running Jewish polemic in which, from at least Paul onwards, Christianity had become a form of paganism. Historical studies have shown convincingly that already by the time of Paul, the early Christians had articulated a belief in Jesus' divinity far more powerfully, and indeed poetically, than anyone had previously imagined. Historical evidence proves conclusively that early *Jewish* Christianity in some way identified Jesus and Israel's God. Moreover, given the emphases of ancient Jewish monotheism, the evidence for early Christian worship of Jesus before the year 50 A.D. was truly an extraordinary and rapid-spreading development. Some scholars hold the astonishing view that essentially more happened to beliefs in and about Jesus within the few years between his bodily resurrection and Paul's first letter than in the entire subsequent 700 years of church history, an opinion to which I subscribe.

A Mysticism of the Holy Spirit

"God's love has been poured out into our hearts through the Holy Spirit." (Rom 5:5)

Once again, what I mean by a mystic is someone who has the consciousness of the immediate or direct presence of God the Father, or Christ, or the Holy Spirit, or of all three. With respect to Paul, I add that in Jesus-Messiah's light, the deepest meaning of the Jewish scriptures were revealed to him, just as Jesus had explained to the Emmaus disciples how the scriptures referred to him.

The Holy Spirit has been called the Cinderella person of the Holy Trinity. Although the word *Spirit* appears roughly 150 times in the New Testament—slightly more than a hundred in Paul's writing—the early Christian major controversies centered around the person of Jesus-Messiah. If Christianity had proclaimed a God consisting of only Father and Son, then the doctrinal conflicts would not have been very different from what they were. The Holy Spirit seems to have been included in the doctrine of God almost as an afterthought about which believers had no strong feelings, either for or against. It is striking that with the exception of what the modified Nicene Creed proclaimed of the Holy Spirit, "who with the Father and the Son together is worshipped and glorified," there are no known prayers to the Holy Spirit until about ten centuries after Jesus' bodily resurrection.

Paul wrote: "For it is we who are the circumcision, we who worship by the Spirit of God, who glory in Christ Jesus, and who put no confidence in the flesh" (Phil 3:3). Perhaps this is the way it should be, namely, that the Holy Spirit calls attention to Jesus-Messiah and not to himself. However, there is some evidence that the Holy Spirit was worshiped early in conjunction with the Father and the Son and that worship was offered not only *through* the Holy Spirit but also *to* the Holy Spirit.

It has already been shown that Paul deliberately wrote of Jesus-Messiah within the framework of Second Temple Jewish monotheism but did not add him to an incipient pantheon. He declared that the identity of the one God of Jewish monotheism had been made known in Jesus' person. This also applies to the Holy Spirit. Paul used the language of this Jewish monotheism and reworked it around Jesus and the Holy Spirit. In addition, the earliest Christians, precisely within their Second Temple Jewish monotheism, unhesitatingly identified Jesus and the Holy Spirit within the one God.

In Paul's Letter to the Romans, he announced:

> Paul, a servant of Christ Jesus, called to be an apostle and set apart for the gospel of God—the gospel he promised beforehand through his prophets in the Holy Scriptures regarding his Son, who as to his earthly life was a descendant of David, and who through the Spirit of holiness was appointed the Son of God in power by his resurrection from the dead: Jesus Christ our Lord. Through him we received grace and apostleship to call all the Gentiles to the obedience that comes from faith for his name's sake. (Rom 1:1–5)

Later on in this epistle, Paul also stressed that:

> because of the grace God gave me to be a minister of Christ Jesus to the Gentiles. He gave me the priestly duty of proclaiming the gospel of God, so that the Gentiles might become an offering acceptable to God, sanctified by the Holy Spirit. Therefore I glory in Christ Jesus in my service to God. I will not venture to speak of anything except what Christ has accomplished through me in leading the Gentiles to obey God by what I have said and done—by the power of signs and wonders, through the power of the Spirit of God. So from Jerusalem all the way around to Illyricum, I have fully proclaimed the gospel of Christ. (Rom 15:15–19)

To the condescending Corinthian community, Paul boldly compared the fruit of his apostolate among them to a letter from Jesus-Messiah, written not with ink, but with the Holy Spirit of the living God on the tablets of human hearts. The synergy between the ministry of the Holy Spirit and its fruit in the church means that the apostle's activity goes beyond his own power and even exceeds his initial understanding of it. Among the ministers whom God called or placed for the entire church were the apostles, whom Paul always puts first. This ministry of the Holy Spirit is therefore predominantly something that has to be carried out by the apostle, who lays the foundation for all else. After these come the prophets. These are followed by different gifts, ministries, ways of acting, or ways of working. Paul described these charisms in reference to the one Holy Spirit, the one Lord, or the one God. More to the point, Paul asserted his Spirit-empowered apostolate when he rebuked the Corinthians for saying about him: "his letters are weighty and forceful, but in person he is unimpressive and his speaking amounts to nothing" (2 Cor 10:10). Paul retorted: "such people should realize that what we are in our letters when we are absent, we will be in our actions when we are present" (2 Cor 10:11).

Paul proudly declared that God qualified him to be an apostle of the new covenant, not of the letter, but of the Holy Spirit. The letter kills but the Holy Spirit gives life. Paul claimed that the inner nature of the gospel itself validated the boldness and freedom of his apostolic and priestly ministry. He reminded the Corinthian cultural snobs that Israel's life was grounded in the Torah and the temple. In the temple dwelt the Shekinah, the glory, the radiance of the one true God that Moses was allowed not only to behold but also actually to reflect. Yes, Paul announced, but that same glory is what is now bestowed through the work of the Holy Spirit—yes, even by way of Paul's strange, shabby, uncouth, uncultured, and apparently humiliating life and work. The contrast Paul drew, however, is not between Moses and himself, but rather between the people who heard Moses and the people here and now who receive his apostolic testimony.

Paul also stressed against his Corinthian opponents that there are different types of spiritual gifts, but the same *Spirit*, different types of service, but the same *Lord*, and different types of activity, but it is the same *God* who instills all of them in everyone. And just as Paul expanded the *Shema* so as to include Jesus within it: "yet for us there is one God, the Father, from whom are all things and for whom we exist, and one Lord, Jesus Christ, through whom are all things and through whom we exist" (1 Cor 8:6), his epistle goes on to write: "all these are the work of one and the same Holy Spirit." All gifts come from the one God—so that now the *Shema* explicitly includes both the Holy Spirit and Jesus. This passage underscores an early and unphilosophical statement of what later scholars would refer to as the metaphysical doctrine of the Trinity. Paul seemed to have thought of it as simply the irreducible three-fullness of the divine work in and among his people, even at the point where he stressed so strongly that in fact it is all the mighty deed of the one God.

Paul understood the Holy Spirit as the one who engendered a sense of God's living presence in the midst of the community, thus enabling Christians to worship, pray, love, and work. And by specifying that those who confess Jesus is Lord do so in the Holy Spirit, Paul undermined any pneumatic elitism to which the Corinthians were prone. In addition, Paul also stressed that Christian hope does not disappoint or cause shame—that hope given from the crucified Messiah—because "the love of God has been poured out into our hearts through the Holy Spirit who has been given to us" (Rom 5:5) and whom we experience. The heart of believers is the place where (and the means by which) they are to love God, according to the *Shema*. Paul also viewed the Holy Spirit as the outpouring of the personal presence and energy of the one true God that enabled his people to do what the *Shema* required: to love God with their whole heart. Thus, Paul presented here—and elsewhere—what might be called a pneumatological monotheism and mysticism.

In Galatians 4, Paul powerfully recasts classical Jewish monotheism to include both Jesus and the Holy Spirit together (Gal 4:4–6). Paul emphasized that the Galatian Christians—already complete in Christ—had no need for the Torah's burden because the God of Abraham and the exodus was now to be known, worshiped, and trusted as the God who sent the Son and the Holy Spirit of the Son. To reinforce his point, Paul wrote of the Galatians as having now come to know the God of the new exodus, or rather to be known by this God, who has destroyed all pagan idols. As he wrote, "Formerly, when you did not know God, you were slaves to those who by nature are not gods. But now that you know God—or rather are known by God—how is it that you are turning back to those weak and miserable forces? (Gal 4:8–9). Thus, the Galatians had entered into a relationship of mutual knowing with this Son-sending and Spirit-sending God who is the one true God—with God taking and retaining the initiative. Galatians is arguably the earliest Christian document we possess. From it, one might conclude that if the doctrine of the Trinity had not come into existence, it would have been necessary to invent it.

This extraordinary chapter in Galatians flows smoothly into another of Paul's epistles, namely Romans, chapter 8, where he again depended heavily on exodus motifs. Set free from slavery, God's people must depend upon God's presence and leadership in order not to be forcibly returned to Egypt. Furthermore, despite their sinful rebellion, the divine glory—God's Shekinah—dwelt in the tabernacle just outside the camp gate. In Paul's retelling of the story, the Holy Spirit takes the place of the divine glory, leading the people to the promised land, which turns out to be *not* heaven—as found in much Christian distortion of the story—but the renewed creation, the cosmos finally liberated from its own slavery, experiencing its own exodus. The Holy Spirit forms the first fruits of the new creation, the sign of the greater harvest to come, consonant with the idea of the initial down payment, which ensures that the rest will be paid at its proper time.

The redemption of human beings occurs not merely for the sake of the rescued humans—important though that is—but also so that, through their new lives, the one God can engender his wise order to redeem the rest of the world. This too is part of typical Jewish monotheism. What the one God of Israel had done in the exodus narrative, and has promised to do again at the eschaton, Paul saw as the Holy Spirit's accomplishment then. So, we see Paul again thinking from within the framework of Jewish-style monotheism. He saw the Holy Spirit alongside the Son as the agent of the one God, doing what Wisdom was to do, doing what the Torah wanted to do, but could not. This is why, to the puzzlement of many Pauline readers throughout the centuries, Paul saw himself writing in strongly positive terms about the Torah—it really was *God's* law, and thus holy, just, and good—while at the same time insisting that the purposes for which the Torah had been given have now been fulfilled and so it is no longer necessary in the new messianic family.

Paul regularly wrote in many ways that indicate that he regarded the Holy Spirit, as he regarded Jesus-Messiah, as a glorious manifestation of Yhwh himself. He dared to write: "now the Lord is the Spirit, and where the Spirit of the Lord is, there is freedom" (2 Cor 3:17). Paul had called both Yhwh and Jesus *Lord,* but here wrote *the Lord is the Spirit,* so much scholarly ink has been spilled over the text's meaning. I share the view of those exegetes who stress that here Paul is calling Yhwh the *Spirit* who appeared to Moses in Exodus 34. The Spirit who was the Lord, Yhwh, is the Lord whose glory was transforming the Corinthians. This text also indirectly states the unity-in-difference between Father, Son, and Holy Spirit. Consonant with various elements of the exodus narrative, the Holy Spirit is the ultimate mode of Yhwh's personal and powerful presence *with*, and even *in*, his people. Thus, the identity of the *one* God must now include Jesus-Messiah and the Holy Spirit—and focused especially on the Jewish eschatology of the return of Yhwh.

Chapter 8 of Paul's Epistle to the Romans is rife with references to the Holy Spirit, which have the same cumulative impact as 2 Corinthians 3. These text call attention to the Holy Spirit as the personal, powerful manifestation of the one God of Jewish monotheism. Paul proclaimed that the law of the Holy Spirit of Life in Jesus-Messiah has set us free from the law of sin and death. Living according to the Holy Spirit (not according to the flesh) with our minds centered on the demands of the Holy Spirit will result in a life of peace because of God's covenant justice. The one who does not have the Holy Spirit dwelling within him does not belong to Jesus-Messiah. If the Holy Spirit of the one who raised Jesus from the dead lives within a person, by the Spirit that person will put to death sinful deeds and will live. The one led by God's Holy Spirit will receive the Spirit of sonship and be able to pray, *Abba, Father*. Having the fruits of the Holy Spirit's life with us, we still groan as we await for adoption as sons. However, the Holy Spirit comes alongside in accord with God's will and helps us in our weakness with intercessions and groanings too deep for words.

The entire passage breathes the very air of Second Temple monotheism. Again, God has done what the Torah could not. Yhwh accomplished in Jesus-Messiah and by the Holy Spirit not only the rescue of humans but also the restoration of creation, breathing his own life-giving Holy Spirit into human nostrils to give life where there was none. And this is the Holy Spirit of both Jesus-Messiah and the Father of the one who raised Jesus bodily from the dead.

One must conclude that Paul did stress that the identities of God, Jesus, and the Holy Spirit are *mutually* constituted by one another—but in an asymmetrical fashion. God the Father is only Father in relation to Jesus as his Son. Insofar as God is the Father who sends and raises his Son, his identity is constituted by that relationship to the Son. But precisely for that reason, the mutuality here is not entirely symmetrical: God is not sent or fathered by Jesus. And Jesus' identity, although constituted in relation to God as his Father, is by the same token constitutive for God's identity. He is God's Son without whom God is not God the Father. Thus, Paul wrote of the full interdependence of

God the Father and Jesus-Messiah on one another for the distinct identities of each, but he did not teach their interchangeability. Again, the mutuality but not the symmetry must be pointed out.

Turning to the Holy Spirit, we find that Paul's way of accounting for mutuality and asymmetry in the relations between God and Jesus provides a template for how to understand the Holy Spirit's relation with both of them as well. The Holy Spirit is the Spirit *of God* and the Spirit *of Jesus-Messiah*. Concomitantly rather than competitively, the identities of God and Jesus are inseparable from the identity and activity of the Holy Spirit. The Holy Spirit is who he is only by virtue of his relations to God and Jesus. Thus, what one finds in Paul's writings must be designated as a nascent trinitarian monotheism and mysticism, a depiction of Israel's God, YHWH, in action fulfilling his ancient promises in an orderly characteristic fashion and doing so not only through but *as* Son and Holy Spirit.

Chapter 5

Paul's Mysticism of Baptism, the Church, and the Eucharist

Paul's Mysticism of Baptism[1]

"We were baptized into one body, by the Holy Spirit." (1 Cor 12:13)

ONE SALIENT ASPECT OF spirituality in some parts of the world centers not on the celebration of the day of one's birth but on the enthusiastic commemoration of one's baptismal day, one's *name day*, usually after the saint of the day, the day on which one became a Christian. I know few Americans who know the date of their baptism. When some of the saints sinned, they would immediately recall their baptism, the initial washing of their souls. Given the emphasis on baptism in the Christian tradition, it is indeed disappointing how few parents in the Western world even bother to have their children baptized and how, in general, this great sacrament is forgotten.

Paul challenged the factionalism and divisions in the Corinthian communities by appealing to baptism: "What I mean is this: One of you says, 'I follow Paul'; another, 'I follow Apollos'; another, 'I follow Cephas'; still another, 'I follow Christ.' Is Christ divided? Was Paul crucified for you? *Were you baptized in the name of Paul?* . . . For Christ did not send me to baptize but to preach the gospel—not with wisdom and eloquence, lest the cross of Christ be emptied of its power" (1 Cor 1:12–17). Paul stressed here that one's community was defined by baptism and that baptism was defined as the entry ritual into the people of Jesus-Messiah. Through baptism *into* the name of the Messiah, one lives in community in

---

1. Wright, *Faithfulness of God*, 417–27, 962–64; Schweitzer, *The Mysticism of Paul*, 230–33, 260–63.

the presence of Jesus-Messiah. Early Christians often referred to baptism as the *mystical waters*.

When Paul declared that Jesus-Messiah did not send him to baptize but to preach the gospel, this is not, despite the natural but anti-sacramental reading in much of Protestantism, a downgrading of baptism by comparison with preaching. It is anachronistic to look for a division in Paul between word and sacrament. Here he also emphasized his own vocation and expressed horror that anything he said might be taken as grounds for the creation of a Paul faction in competition with the only genuine group, that of the one community of Jesus-Messiah.

To comprehend much in Paul's letters, one must understand his worldview: the Jewish scriptures—but rethought in the light of the crucified and risen Jesus-Messiah and the Holy Spirit. For example, the exodus story formed the salient backdrop to his mysticism of baptism. It bound together the single community and fellowship with the one God, the one Lord, and the one Holy Spirit—again, a proto-trinitarian community. We read: "For I do not want you to be ignorant of the fact, brothers and sisters, that our ancestors were all under the cloud and that they all passed through the sea. They were all baptized into Moses in the cloud and in the sea. They all ate the same spiritual food and drank the same spiritual drink; for they drank from the spiritual rock that accompanied them, and that rock was Christ" (1 Cor 10:1–4). The double use of water in this passage—the water of the Red Sea through which the Israelites passed and the water that flowed from the rock for them to drink in the desert—is easily explained for the otherwise puzzling double reference in chapter 12: "For we were all baptized by one Spirit so as to form one body—whether Jews or Gentiles, slave or free—and we were all given the one Spirit to drink" (1 Cor 12:13). The redeeming action on Israel's behalf by the holy presence of the one God in their midst, leading them by the pillar of cloud and fire and sustaining them on their journey, now came from Jesus-Messiah. As a result, they were the *new exodus* people, formed as was ancient Israel, into a new people through baptism.

Paul highlighted baptism as the visible sign of entry into Jesus-Messiah's people—defining them just as surely as the crossing of the Red Sea defined the people whom Abraham's God brought out of Egypt. In short, baptism was the visible rite of Paul's *into*-Jesus-Messiah mysticism. The basic point was that the baptismal action, resonating with the ancient story of exodus and now reworked around Jesus in the Holy Spirit, bound the baptized to the one God and constituted them as an actual—not merely a theoretical or invisible—community. In so doing, Paul differed greatly from his culture. One entered into the followers of Jesus-Messiah by the rite of baptism. By contrast, no ritual was needed for either a native-born Roman or a non-Roman foreigner in order to belong to the divine and human solidarity of the Roman community and to participate in the celebrations required to sustain the civic life of the city.

I do not share the position of those scholars who link Paul's emphasis on baptism to the Greek mystery religions of his day. Paul's "into-Christ-mysticism" through baptism is definitely his transformed Judaism, consonant with the Jewish stress on the exodus narrative and its significance. Also, Jewish proselyte washings do not serve as a sufficient analogy for Paul's view of baptism. Some scholars trace Paul's baptism back to John the Baptist, who in turn depended on the prophet Ezekiel: "I will sprinkle clean water on you, and you will be clean; I will cleanse you from all your impurities and from all your idols. I will give you a new heart and put a new spirit in you; I will remove from you your heart of stone and give you a heart of flesh. And I will put my Spirit in you and move you to follow my decrees and be careful to keep my laws" (Ezek 36:25–27). Which begs the question: what was both Ezekiel's and John's source? Again, it was the exodus event. John the Baptist's baptism evoked the exodus. And he believed that Israel's God was calling out a new, renewed people and that YHWH himself would shortly appear in person in their midst. To some extent Paul saw an analogy between baptism and circumcision: "In him you were also circumcised with a circumcision not performed by human hands. Your whole self, ruled by the flesh was put off when you were circumcised by Christ" (Col 2:11–12).

However, Paul's mysticism of incorporation into Jesus' death and resurrection loomed far larger in his understanding of baptism. His Epistle to the Romans frequently stresses baptism in relation to Jesus-Messiah's death and resurrection. One example must suffice: "we were therefore buried with him through baptism into death in order that, just as Christ was raised from the dead through the glory of the Father, we too may live a new life" (Rom 6:4). And Paul understood this as a real happening—and not just figuratively.

In Romans 6, Paul once again explained baptism in terms of a much larger redrawn exodus narrative. Baptism sets slaves free, that is, free from the yoke of sin. Paul's view that SIN, DEATH, and SATAN are intrinsically linked should be emphasize, and it is worth observing that his view of SIN, DEATH, and SATAN as a domain is a far cry from contemporary banal notions of what sin actually is.

This chapter places baptism in the context of the gift and presence of the Holy Spirit. The exodus narrative focused on the living presence of YHWH who accompanied his people out of Egypt and came to dwell in the tabernacle, the forerunner of the Jerusalem temple. Only when the exodus story is brought out from the shadows of this background and placed in Paul's spotlight can we understand where his idea of a required initiation rite for entering the Jesus-Messiah community comes from. Paul's revolutionary view of both baptism and of community proclaims that since we are all baptized into the name of Jesus-Messiah, we are likewise baptized into his body. "Just as a body, though one, has many parts, but all its many parts form one body, so it is with Christ. For we were all baptized by one Spirit so as to form one body—whether Jews or Gentiles, slave or free—and we were all given the one Spirit to drink" (1 Cor 12:12–13).

Paul did not consider baptism primarily as something done to the individual but as the ritual that defined the community of the baptized as the people of Jesus-Messiah. Those who submit to baptism are thereby challenged to learn the way of life that this community is committed to precisely because it is the family of the crucified and risen Messiah. Jews and Greeks, slave and free, male and female (one might add people of all races, colors, and cultures) became the *united* nature of the family defined by baptism in*to* the Messiah. Again, Paul's understanding of baptism centered upon the single-family, the one community, rooted in his messianic monotheism shaped around Jesus himself and his Holy Spirit .

As one would expect, pagans—hostile to Jesus and his followers—cursed Jesus. Thus, Paul wrote: "You know that when you were pagans, somehow or other you were influenced and led astray to mute idols. Therefore, I want you to know that no one who is speaking by the Spirit of God says, 'Jesus be cursed,' and no one can say, 'Jesus is Lord,' except by the Holy Spirit" (1 Cor 12:2–3). Instead of the ecstatic utterances of pagan worship, Christian worship provides the ecstatic utterance, "Jesus is Lord." Obviously quite different spirits animate the ones who cursed Jesus, on the one hand, and those who joyfully hailed him as *the Lord* and the name above every name, on the other. The work of the Holy Spirit was precisely to bind worshipers to Jesus-Messiah in exultant communion. The one God shares in the common life of this new community and this new community participates in the life of the divine: the same Spirit, the same Lord, the same God, engendering everything in everyone.

This view is precisely what religion meant in the ancient world of Paul's day—except that it is now all reorganized around Jesus-Messiah and the Holy Spirit. Any intelligent Roman hearing all this would say, "This is indeed religion, though it is quite different from anything we have imagined or experienced in our world." Paul was writing about a new body, a new kind of civic community, in which precisely the normal distinctions by which civic life were marked—ethnic and social classes—were now irrelevant. Through baptism, people became those in whom the Holy Spirit now dwells—living temples. The reason the first Christians needed the baptismal rite of initiation was not because they were inventing a new mystery religion but because they believed that the new exodus had occurred and with it new creation. Entering the renewed people of Jesus-Messiah through baptism was extremely important for Paul and his churches. In the light of his Jewish worldview, he perceived that YHWH's covenant with Israel and the exodus narrative, reconfigured around Jesus, provided the rationale for such an initiation ritual.

The reason Paul needed to underscore entering, not only with baptism but also his whole theology of justification, was *not* that he was constructing a new religion in parallel with Judaism, but that he believed that the one God had at last done the new thing he had promised. So, the radical nature of this new event demanded a fresh start for all. What Paul believed about YHWH's people, on the basis of what he believed about Jesus-Messiah, demanded that he teach and practice the rite of baptism. Thus, Paul demanded, in the *name* of the Lord Jesus-Messiah "that all agree with one another in what you say and that there be no divisions among you, but that you be perfectly united in mind and thought" (1 Cor 1:10). This emphasis on the name of Jesus-Messiah bore a likeness to the importance in pagan religions—which Paul definitely abjured—of getting the right name when addressing or invoking a God. Also the point of being baptized into the *name* of Jesus-Messiah was intimately linked with Jesus' cross and the transformed *Shema*: one God, one Lord, one Holy Spirit.

Behind this stood the strange words of Jesus himself, subsequently interpreted by his disciples in the light of the events of his passion, crucifixion, death, and resurrection. Jesus had spoken cryptically of the *baptism* with which he had to be baptized—nothing less than his death. The confluence of these events—Jesus' passion, crucifixion, death, and resurrection—and a retrospective rethinking of Jesus' baptism at the start of his public career, which had taken place precisely at the time of the Passover, meant that the history, story, and prophetic symbolism rushed together with tremendous force. Jesus-Messiah did nothing less than bring Israel's history to perfection. Jesus' followers believed that the new age had been launched by his resurrection and the gift of his Holy Spirit. Thus, baptism retained the meaning it had during Jesus' public career: identification with his kingdom movement—thy kingdom come *on earth*. This also deepened baptism's resonance with the Israelite exodus and with Jesus' death. Baptism gave rise to the unity of the church and its holiness.

Paul expressed his salient understanding about baptism this way: "Don't you know that all of us who were baptized into Christ Jesus were baptized into his death? We were therefore buried with him through baptism into death in order that, just as Christ was raised from the dead through the glory of the Father, we too may live a new life. For if we have been united with him in a death like his, we will certainly also be united with him in a resurrection like his" (Rom 6:3–5). Also, sin no longer ruled because "where sin increased, grace increased all the more" (Rom 5:20). Consequently, through Paul, baptism gained its meaning from two primary poles around which it resolved: the exodus on the one hand and the death and resurrection of Jesus on the other. Paul regarded it as the God-given means by which people would enter into new solidarity, unity, the new humanity whose primary characteristic was that it had been freed from sin by death and resurrection. This meant that a Christian's primary obligation must include holiness. Paul's logic was: you have been baptized, therefore, God is challenging you to die to sin and live the resurrected life. This is Paul's version of religion: Judaism brought to completion.

Vicarious baptism indicates how important baptism was for some of Jesus' earliest followers. The tantalizing text, "what do people mean by being baptized on behalf of the dead? If the dead are not raised at all, why are people baptized on their behalf?" (1 Cor 15:29), has been interpreted in myriad ways. I find myself consonant with those commentators who hold that some of the relatives or friends of catechumens who had died before baptism had themselves been baptized on their behalf—but not that Paul is putting his stamp of approval on this practice. In addition, vicarious baptism is thus analogous to what Paul wrote in 1 Corinthians 7:14: "for the unbelieving husband has been sanctified through his wife, and the unbelieving wife has been sanctified through her believing husband.

Otherwise your children would be unclean, but as it is, they are holy." This position definitely contradicted Jewish views of what was considered holy and what was viewed as unclean.

In addition, Paul pointed out to the Corinthian deniers of the resurrection that if there is no resurrection, why bother to be baptized on behalf of the dead? Why should he or anyone in the community suffer so much for the gospel based on bodily resurrection, if there is none? The next verse calls attention to his apostolate, "and as for us, why do we endanger ourselves every hour? I face death every day—yes, just as surely as I boast about you in Christ Jesus our Lord. If I fought wild beasts in Ephesus with no more than human hopes, what have I gained? If the dead are not raised, 'Let us eat and drink, for tomorrow we die'" (1 Cor 15:30–32). To clinch his argument, Paul stressed: "For if the dead are not raised, then Christ has not been raised either. And if Christ has not been raised, your faith is futile; you are still in your sins. Then those also who have fallen asleep in Christ are lost. If only for this life we have hope in Christ, we are of all people most to be pitied" (1 Cor 15:16–19).

Paul's Mysticism of the Church

"Saul, Saul, why do you persecute me?" (Acts 9:4)

I have already emphasized that persecuting Jesus' followers loomed in Paul's mind as his most regrettable sin. I contend that the foundation of Paul's mysticism of the church centered on what Jesus asked on the Damascus road: "Saul, Saul! Why do you persecute *me*?" The Hebrew word *qahal* designated the congregation of Israel that YHWH assembled during her wilderness experience. The Greek scriptures—the Septuagint—translated the Hebrew word *qahal* as *ekklesia*, found sixty-two times in Paul's letters. In essence, Paul's ecclesial mysticism resulted from his realization that Jesus-Messiah lived in those who believed in him. He identified those baptized into Jesus-Messiah's death and resurrection as in some way identical with Christ. What you do to *them*, you do to *him*—such is Paul's view of mystical union, mystical incorporation, the mystical concorporation that exists between Jesus-Messiah and his followers.

The people of faith defined Jesus-Messiah's community through a faith that specifically confessed Jesus as Lord and believed that the one God raised Jesus bodily from the dead. Paul made no split between faith and faithfulness, as modern Christians often do, so to him faith in Jesus was faithfulness to Jesus and was akin to the Messiah's own faith in/faithfulness to the God of Israel and his purposes. In any case, the actual content of both Pauline faith and faithfulness is the death and resurrection of Jesus-Messiah himself.

One finds in Paul's epistles a blend of the plural *churches* and the singular *church*—the many forming the one. Thus the ambiguity of using the terms "local" or "particular" relative to "church." He was initially concerned with particular churches in specific locations and only later focused on the transregional church dispersed throughout the Mediterranean basin. During his apostolate and after his death, a variety of *house churches* arose in different Christian mission areas: one house church of Christian *Jews* who still adhered to the Mosaic law but for whom Jesus was the promised Messiah; one house church of *Jewish and gentile* Christians stemming from the mission associated with the Jerusalem apostles and honoring the Twelve as founders; another house church from the Pauline mission, consisting mostly of *gentiles* who saw themselves as free of the Jewish law.

Paul eventually regarded the church as something universal and celestial, the temple of heaven, Jesus-Messiah's heavenly bride. The church goes to heaven with the risen Christ. Thus, the body of Christ, the church, is his glorified body, fully empowered by the Holy Spirit. She is the summit of God's sanctifying power in Jesus-Messiah. One might also say that, for Paul, since Christ is the temple of God, then the church as the body of Christ is the temple of God and that the divine Spirit of Wisdom indwells the church-as-temple. As a result, divine Wisdom indwells us as the Spirit to make us church-as-temple.

Paul's use of the phrase "the church of God" invites a comparison between the Israelite wilderness community and the community of those called in Jesus-Messiah. Paul understood the church as both a continuation and the fulfillment of the old Israel, God's own chosen people. When viewed in the light of the Holy Spirit, the church was also a new nation, the new Israel, the ultimate Passover family—as opposed to the flesh that was the old nation. God had Jesus-Messiah's new community in mind when he promised Abraham that he would form a great nation from his seed and bless all the earth's families through him. Paul emphasized that those who belong to the Messiah are of *Abraham's seed*, heirs according to God's promise. Paul's mystically rethought *monotheism* grounded his understanding of the *single* united community, a single covenantal family. Because God is *one*, that single family must be *one* through *Abraham's single seed*. Paul likewise rethought this view in the light of Jesus himself, the messianic representation of Israel, as the seed promised to Abraham. One might likewise speak of Paul's *seed*, because he wrote: "for in Christ Jesus I became your father through the gospel" (1 Cor 4:14).

In his Letter to the Romans, Paul asked: "is God the God of Jews only? Is he not the God of Gentiles too? Yes, of Gentiles too" (Rom 3:29). Standing firm on the *Shema* itself that proclaims the one God, Paul argued for one united church. However, he shifted the Jewish view of Israel away from itself to a larger, worldwide family based on faith in Jesus-Messiah, not the Torah. Paul highlighted the *one* church as God's true heir in Jesus-Messiah. The church of Jerusalem, which was the nucleus of the universal church, inherited the title from its Jewish ancestors, and so it came to be applied to the entire church. However, the Jerusalem Christians had monopolized certain terms inherited from the old Israel: *community of God*, the *saints*, and the *elect*. Paul would have rejected such distinctions within the church, and we can imagine that he would have had no time for the much later opinion, still current among many, that God willed three churches: the Roman Catholic church, the Eastern Orthodox church, and the Protestant churches. There is only one church.

Paul's Letter to Philemon offers a salient example of how his encounter with Jesus on the Damascus road revolutionized his view of the Messiah's community, the church.[2] Imprisoned in Ephesus, but calling himself "a prisoner of king Jesus," Paul wrote to his convert Philemon concerning the converted slave Onesimus, who had come to him for advice. It should be noted that Paul did not refer to the slave Onesimus as a fugitive but as Paul's "beloved son" and therefore Philemon's "beloved brother." In sending him back to Philemon, Paul stressed that he was, "sending him—who is my very heart—back to you . . . no longer as a slave, but better than a slave, as a dear brother. He is very dear to me but even dearer to you, both as a fellow man and as a brother in the Lord" (Phlm 1:12–16).

Moreover, Paul requested that Philemon receive Onesimus as he would receive *Paul himself*, "welcome him as you would welcome me" (Phlm 1:17). However, contrary to popular opinion, Paul was not a proto-abolitionist. The point of the letter is not the freeing of slaves but the underscoring of the equality of everyone in Christ. Treating a slave as a beloved *brother* sounds radical to some people even to this day.

2. Wright, *Fidelity of God*, 3–74.

For Paul, the reconciliation and mutual welcome of all those in the Messiah took precedence over everything else, including requesting Philemon to set Onesimus free. As much as Paul valued freedom, the mutual reconciliation of those who belonged to Jesus-Messiah mattered more than anything else. Paul was actually embodying what he elsewhere called the ministry of reconciliation. He announced: "All this is from God, who reconciled us to himself through Christ and gave us the ministry of reconciliation: that God was reconciling the world to himself in Christ, not counting people's sins against them. And he has committed to us the message of reconciliation. We are therefore Christ's ambassadors, as though God were making his appeal through us. We implore you on Christ's behalf: Be reconciled to God" (2 Cor 5:18–20). Paul's apostolic ministry embraced both Philemon, the slave owner, and Onesimus, the slave, as brothers in Jesus-Messiah—that is what the ministry of reconciliation was.

Still, when Paul continued, "knowing that you will do even more than I ask" (Phlm 1:21), this does hint at manumission. Perhaps he had Deuteronomy in mind, "Remember that you were slaves in Egypt and the LORD your God redeemed you" (Deut 15:15). Undoubtedly, the actual situation in Paul's day was somewhat different from ours—freed slaves were by no means always better off. Paul did indeed want Onesimus back as a coworker, and was hinting at emancipation. However, Paul's main point highlights the issues of mutual reconciliation that points beyond the small horizons of his letter to a larger worldview upon which Paul depended.

Paul's letter to the Galatians made an even sharper point: "So in Christ Jesus you are all children of God through faith, for all of you who were baptized into Christ have clothed yourselves with Christ. There is neither Jew nor Gentile, neither slave nor free, nor is there male and female, for you are all one in Christ Jesus. If you belong to Christ, then you are Abraham's seed, and heirs according to the promise" (Gal 3:25–29). Given the era in which Paul lived, what he announced here is truly revolutionary. For our times, Paul would have added: "neither people of all colors and races."

In this way, Paul expressed the obligation to welcome one another that must exist between two or more members of the messianic family. At the heart of Paul's work was the yearning and striving for messianic unity across traditional boundaries, whether it be the unity of Jew and gentile in the Messiah, the unity of the church under the Lordship of Jesus-Messiah in a pagan imperial context, or as even the unity of master and slave—expressing again what it means to be *in Christ*. As a result, the main thrust in

Galatians stressed that all who have this faith belonged in the same, single community, eating at the same, single table. *This* is what Paul meant by the much disputed term *justification by faith*.

As a result of further revelations and Paul's own reflections, he came to comprehend the church as the body of the crucified and risen Messiah in the sense of a mystical Jesus-Messiah, although he never used the term *mystical body*.[3] The body of Jesus-Messiah can refer to Jesus' crucified body or to his eucharistic body, but in 1 Corinthians 12 Paul clearly related it to the Corinthian church: "Just as a body, though one, has many parts, but all its many parts form one body, so it is with Christ. For we were all baptized by one Spirit so as to form one body—whether Jews or Gentiles, slave or free—and we were all given the one Spirit to drink" (1 Cor 12:12–14). If one member suffers, all suffer together. As Paul wrote: "Now you are the body of Christ, and each one of you is a part of it. And God has placed in the church first of all apostles, second prophets, third teachers, then miracles, then gifts of healing, of helping, of guidance, and of different kinds of tongues" (1 Cor 12:27–28). The word *church* in this text has *universal* overtones and the *one* body of Jesus-Messiah required the need for diversity. Thus, Paul listed the different ministries and charisms that God has appointed for the church. As members of Christ's body, each has a different function intended for the common good.

Paul's understanding of the church as the body of Jesus-Messiah was hardly abstract because he used the term to respond to certain problems plaguing the Corinthian community. He warned that participation in the table of the Lord and the table of demons were mutually exclusive. *Idolatry*—not sins in the contemporary sense—marked Israel's history. Because one shared the one body of Christ in the Eucharist, the one bread also made the many one body. Paul also rebuked the fractious Corinthian groups when he wrote: "some from Chloe's household have informed me that there are quarrels among you. What I mean is this: One of you says, 'I follow Paul'; another, 'I follow Apollos'; another, 'I follow Cephas'; still another, 'I follow Christ.' Is Christ divided? Was Paul crucified for you? Were you baptized in the name of Paul?" (1 Cor 1:11–13). Also, because they were members of the church whose bodies were members of Jesus-Messiah, not only refraining from immorality but also living a life of love as found in Paul's classic description of love found in his first Epistle to the Corinthians (1 Cor 13) should be obvious.

3. De Lubac, *Corpus Mysticum*.

Paul's Epistles to the Colossians and to the Ephesians developed the imagery of the body in new ways. In these, he focused on Jesus-Messiah as the head of the body, which is the church, whose growth he nourishes. For instance, he wrote: "he [Jesus-Messiah] is the head of the body, the church" (Col 1:18). Paul likewise combined the head and body metaphor with the marriage metaphor. Comparing the relationship of Jesus-Messiah and his church to the relationship of husband and wife, because Jesus loved the church and handed himself over for her to make her holy, the church should be subject to Christ. Christ nourishes and cares for the church as a man cares for his own body (Eph 5:25–28). Thus, Paul came to the realization that ekklesia should also refer to the one church universally spread throughout the world. God has subjected all things to Christ and made him head over all things for the sake of the church, which is the body of Christ. For example, Paul wrote, "God placed all things under his feet and appointed him to be head over everything for the church" (Eph 1:22). Christ, in turn, has created the new humanity in himself so that he might reconcile Jew and gentile in one body through the blood of the cross. He proclaimed: "For God was pleased to have all his fullness dwell in [Jesus-Messiah], and through him to reconcile to himself all things, whether things on earth or things in heaven, by making peace through his blood, shed on the cross" (Col 1:19–20).

Thus, the church is the showpiece of Jesus-Messiah's work of reconciliation. The fullness of Jesus-Messiah fills all things with God's fullness. And through it God reveals the mystery hidden for ages, but now revealed to the holy apostles and prophets, that the gentiles have become fellow heirs, members of the same body, and sharers in the promise of Jesus-Messiah through the gospel. Aware that those who were in Jesus-Messiah had been called, elected, sanctified, and set apart for worship in the Holy Spirit, Paul also denoted the Christian community as the *temple of God* because God's Holy Spirit dwells in it. For instance, he wrote: "Don't you know that you yourselves are God's temple and that God's Spirit dwells in your midst?" (1 Cor 3:16). God's Holy Spirit, God's glorious Shekinah presence, had left the temple when the Babylonians sacked Jerusalem and took the Israelites into exile. Now both the individual Christian and the Christian community have become the Holy Spirit's new abode and a sign that the exile was over. Thus, as the temple of the living God, believers were as different from unbelievers as light was from darkness—and must live accordingly.

Christians must remind themselves that they were now citizens of heaven (Phil 3:18) with the saints and also members of the household of God. Built on the foundation of the apostles and prophets, Jesus-Messiah being the cornerstone, they grow into a holy temple in the Lord (Eph 2:20). Also because one of Israel's privileges was genuine worship of the one true God, Paul understood the Christian community as God's new temple of God. The community members were themselves the spiritual priesthood in the new sanctuary, with their transformed lives being the sweet smelling sacrifice (Eph 5:1–2).

The church focused on unity, holiness, and witness. One can make a good case for seeing Paul's primary aim as the social practice of his communities. He exhorted them to bring their thinking into line with one another and to love, as he described classically in 1 Corinthians 13. He also exhorted them to bring their innermost lives into harmony and to regard everyone else as their superior. Paul insisted that his attitude should be their attitude:

> Though I am free and belong to no one, I have made myself a slave to everyone, to win as many as possible. To the Jews I became like a Jew, to win the Jews. To those under the law I became like one under the law (though I myself am not under the law), so as to win those under the law. To those not having the law I became like one not having the law (though I am not free from God's law but am under Christ's law), so as to win those not having the law. To the weak I became weak, to win the weak. I have become all things to all people so that by all possible means I might save some. (1 Cor 9:19–22)

Even Paul admitted that in so doing, he could only "save some." When he wrote "I became a Jew," should not one interject, but you are a Jew? However, he would have retorted that his identity was not ethnically determined. His found then his own deepest identity in Jesus-Messiah himself. All else is rubbish. Here is the gospel as vocation: "I live, not I, but Jesus-Messiah lives in me."

Paul's Mysticism of the Eucharist

"For as often as you eat this bread and drink this cup, you proclaim the Lord's death until he comes." (1 Cor 11:25)

Everything said so far about exodus, baptism, and sacrifice comes into a new focus when Paul wrote of the breaking of the bread, the Eucharist, the mystical sacrifice of Jesus' body and blood. This shared sacrificial meal is anchored firmly in the exodus story, the Passover narrative, which Jesus-Messiah brought to a shocking fulfillment. Understood as the intimate sharing of life and presence between the Lord and his people, Jesus-Messiah's meal designated the unity, solidarity, and holiness of the community—mystical themes so dear to Paul. This Jewish tradition and ritual, mystical Pasch, now refocused on Jesus-Messiah, far transcended the sacrificial meals of pagan worship and definitely did not replicate the social hierarchy embodied in them.

In 1 Corinthians 10 Paul warned the community not to behave like the idolatrous Israelites in the wilderness. He wrote:

> For I do not want you to be ignorant of the fact, brothers and sisters, that our ancestors were all under the cloud and that they all passed through the sea. They were all baptized into Moses in the cloud and in the sea. They all ate the same spiritual food and drank the same spiritual drink; for they drank from the spiritual rock that accompanied them, and that rock was Christ. Nevertheless, God was not pleased with most of them; their bodies were scattered in the wilderness. Now these things occurred as examples to keep us from setting our hearts on evil things as they did. Do not be idolaters, as some of them were; as it is written: "The people sat down to eat and drink and got up to indulge in revelry." We should not commit sexual immorality, as some of them did—and in one day twenty-three thousand of them died. We should not test Christ, as some of them did—and were killed by snakes. And do not grumble, as some of them did—and were killed by the destroying angel. (1 Cor 10:1–10)

Thus, Paul aligned the crossing of the Red Sea with baptism and the wilderness feedings with the Eucharist. Baptized into Moses, in the cloud, in the Red Sea, they all ate the same spiritual food and drink. Strikingly, Paul permitted Christians to eat meat that had been sacrificed to idols—as long as that did not wound the conscience of those weaker in the faith. Of course, he forbade going to the idol temples to share in pagan meals.

How can sharing in the life of demonic nothings have anything to do with sharing in the life of Jesus-Messiah who vanquished all such non-entities on the cross? Idolatry, not sin in the contemporary sense, had long been Israel's salient temptation. Thus, Paul wrote:

> Therefore, my dear friends, flee from idolatry. I speak to sensible people; judge for yourselves what I say. Is not the cup of thanksgiving for which we give thanks a participation in the blood of Christ? And is not the bread that we break a participation in the body of Christ? Because there is one loaf, we, who are many, are one body, for we all share the one loaf. Consider the people of Israel: Do not those who eat the sacrifices participate in the altar? Do I mean then that food sacrificed to an idol is anything, or that an idol is anything? No, but the sacrifices of pagans are offered to demons, not to God, and I do not want you to be participants with demons. (1 Cor 10:14–20)

Paul reminded the Corinthian Christians that the shared cup of blessing is a sharing in Jesus-Messiah's blood. The broken bread is an actual sharing in Jesus-Messiah's body, so those who participate at the Lord's table are actually sharing the Jesus-Messiah's own life. There is one loaf. Hence, they become one body because of the sharing of the one loaf. Paul's salient point is the sharing of common life. The exodus context thus led Paul directly and naturally to the intimate sharing of life and presence between the Lord Jesus and his people.

Paul further rebuked the Corinthians for turning the Lord's Supper into a travesty. He wrote: "So then, when you come together, it is not the Lord's Supper you eat, for when you are eating, some of you go ahead with your own private suppers. As a result, one person remains hungry and another gets drunk. Don't you have homes to eat and drink in? Or do you despise the church of God by humiliating those who have nothing? What shall I say to you? Shall I praise you? Certainly not in this matter!" (1 Cor 11:20–22). In the ancient world, the distinction of class and wealth dominated even more so than it often does in our world. This contradicted Paul's entire vision of the one church, where all are one in Jesus-Messiah.

Paul declared in 1 Cor 11:29 that if people eat and drink *without recognizing the body* they are eating and drinking judgment on themselves—"For those who eat and drink without discerning the body of Christ eat and drink judgment on themselves." His mysticism of Christian incorporation or con-corporation into the crucified and risen body of Jesus-Messiah meant that the body in this context is the united community, Jesus-Messiah's single family. Thus, social divisions turned the Lord's Supper into a farce. Paul demanded that they treat each other as honored guests by waiting for each other (1 Cor 11:33). Why? The Corinthians must recognize the body in the sense that they who eat and drink this meal are a single body. There may be several of them but they are one body because they all share the one loaf.

An amusing Australian theologian friend quipped that had Paul not written about the Lord's Supper, German biblical scholars would have denied that he knew anything about it. True, and I find remarkable Paul's statement that his knowledge of the Lord's Supper did *not* come from the Christian community but: "what I *received from the Lord* and handed on to you" (1 Cor 11:23, my emphasis). One finds in Paul a Jesus-Messiah mystically given revelation and its handing on![4] This is the language of both mysticism and tradition that to this day has been deeply suspect in Protestant circles but was no problem for Paul.

Paul assumed not only that the Eucharist was central to the worshiping life of the Corinthians, but that it also summed up the events that led to Jesus' death—on the night when he was betrayed. It likewise symbolized his forthcoming sacrifice on the cross. Paul claimed that eating Jesus' body and drinking his blood is much more than simply an aid to memory ("do this in memory of me"). He viewed the Lord's Supper by looking both backwards and forwards. This key ritual announces the Lord's death *until he comes*. Hence, the present time got its meaning by making a past event into a here-and-now reality that anticipated the future. The Lord's presence permeated past, present, and future.

It followed from this that anyone who eats the bread or drinks the cup of the Lord unworthily by not recognizing the united community will incur the Lord's judgment and be punished. Anything that fragments the unity of the Lord's single body is a crime against the Lord himself. Hence, in Paul's view, the Lord's Supper was a ritual founded on an actual

---

4. Some exegetes understand this text as Paul presenting himself as a link in the chain of tradition reaching back to Jesus, whose authority remains present in the church. They also stress that Paul's version of the words of institution is closest to that of Luke, but not dependent upon it. I maintain, however, that if this view were correct, Paul would have expressed himself on this point more in terms of 1 Cor 15:3, "For what I received I passed on to you." One might argue that Paul was aware of the traditional words of institution in the light of his Christ-consciousness, thus a genuine revelation sparked by tradition.

event in which the worshipers shared the life of the divinity being worshiped: paradoxically, a human being recently crucified whose death was understood as a sacrifice. This ritual action must bind the community together, so that signs of disunity during it are a contradiction of its inner meaning and will have bad consequences for that community. Any pagan who heard and grasped what Paul described here would conclude that this ritual was indeed part of a religion, even though it was quite unlike anything that had been imagined before. In the same way, any Jewish onlooker would have seen that Israel's traditions, particularly the narrative of the exodus, had provided the framework for Paul's understanding. But again, no Jew before Jesus-Messiah's time had imagined anything quite like this. Again, this is *Judaism fulfilled*.

I witnessed a discussion between two biblical scholars. One argued that Paul's exhortation to recognizing the body referred to the united community. The other argued that it meant recognizing the crucified and risen Jesus. The false dichotomy presented by those scholars failed to grasp that the head cannot be separated from the body. Is not the community incorporated—one body—with Jesus' risen and crucified body? Mover, Paul's text is clear: "Is not the cup of thanksgiving for which we give thanks a participation in *the blood of Christ*? And is not the bread that we break a participation in *the body of Christ*? Because there is one loaf, we, who are many, are one body, for we all share the one loaf?" (1 Cor 10:14–19, my emphasis). So, I contend that Paul wanted the Jesus-Messiah people to recognize *both* the transformed Jesus-Messiah's body *and* blood and the one Jesus-Messiah community.

Sacrifice happened all the time in every city in the Greco-Roman world in Paul's day. One was never far away either from an animal about to be killed, or from the smell of a recently sacrificed animal being cooked and eaten. The city state was bound together by such things, just as individuals were bound thereby to the specific gods with whom they were hoping to do business. This primary obligation of animal sacrifice was to be done over and over again to ensure that the agricultural basis for human life would be blessed and assured of fruitful continuation and that the gods and humans could live together in harmony and solidarity.

Although the early Christians—unlike their pagan counterparts—offered no animal sacrifices, Paul was not shy about using the language of sacrifice and even priesthood to address the primary obligation of those in Christ. He exhorted them to offer their bodies, that is, their whole self to the one God. He exhorted them: "Therefore, I urge you, brothers and sisters, in view of God's mercy, to offer your bodies as a living sacrifice, holy and pleasing to God—this is your true and proper worship. Do not conform to the pattern of this world, but be transformed by the renewing of your mind. Then you will be able to test and approve what God's will is— his good, pleasing, and perfect will" (Rom 12:1–2). This is beyond dispute technical language for presenting a sacrifice.

Paul shocked the Corinthian Christians by proclaiming to them that *they* are the *temple* of God, the *sacrifice itself, and* the *priest* offering sacrifice. This was religion all right: *sacrifice, worship,* and the *knitting together* thereby of a single community and fellowship one with another and especially with the God being worshiped. Paul understood that those in Jesus-Messiah as the sacrificial event of the new age needed a transformed mind and heart. This demanded that the body, the whole public person, was offered as a sacrifice to the one God. The death that took place in baptism was now matched by the resurrection to new life. The newly allied person belonging to God was to be offered to God and to be available for worship and work. (It is often forgotten that a Christian ordained priesthood arose only after the Jerusalem temple was destroyed. Especially in Jewish Christian households, the host would have been the woman head of the house. However, to use the word *presider* would be anachronistic.)

Paul also stressed: "For God was pleased to have all his fullness dwell in him, and through him to reconcile to himself all things, whether things on earth or things in heaven, by making peace through his blood, shed on the cross" (Col 1:19–20). Thus, contrary to Luther, sacrifice is not something humans do to earn favor with God—in other words, part of so-called works-righteousness. Jesus' bloody sacrifice on the cross and the eucharistic meal sacrifice were analogous to the peace offerings depicted in the Jewish scriptures. There was no angry pagan God demanding sacrifice to gain his favor. After the priest killed the animal, its blood, the symbol of life, was poured on the altar—the place where heaven and earth meet. This highlighted that all life belongs to God. The blood was then sprinkled on the people to stress that life was God's gift to his people.

Note that the blood removed the people's sins, not the killing of the animal. Some of the meat was given to the priest and the rest eaten by the people in a communal meal—this foreshadowed the eucharistic meal-sacrifice. Of course, blood is a symbol of life and blood is love made visible. In the context of the peace offering, it emphasizes the one blood, the one life, shared between God and his people. Also, the sacrifice that Paul describes in Romans 12 was to take place in the context of the mercies of God. He understood sacrifice in that context. Paul's view of Israel's peace offerings was a far cry from the pagan view of sacrifice as placating a wrathful god. In fact, he expressed his own apostolate and that of Christians in explicitly sacrificial terms.

He proclaimed: "Yet I have written you quite boldly on some points to remind you of them again, because of the grace God gave me to be a minister of Christ Jesus to the Gentiles. He gave me the *priestly* duty of proclaiming the gospel of God, so that the Gentiles might become an offering acceptable to God, sanctified by the Holy Spirit" (Rom 15:15–16, my emphasis). He confessed that, "because of the grace that God has given me to enable me to be a minister of king Jesus for the nations, working in the priestly service of God's good news, so that the offering of the nations may be acceptable, sanctified by the Holy Spirit." He also announced: "But even if I am being poured out like a drink offering on the sacrifice and service coming from your faith, I am glad and rejoice with all of you" (Phil 2:17). In this letter, Paul was specially conscious of the Roman imperial context. Celebrations meant festivals, processions, garlands of flowers, street parties, games, and athletic contests. Celebration meant above all sacrifice. At the height of the event, the participants would end up in the temple of whatever god was hosting the festivities and there animals were slaughtered and offered up, with all the trimmings—including libations of wine poured on top of the sacrifice.

Paul understood his apostolate to the gospel and the active faith of the Philippian Christians as being like that—a celebration. The heart of it was a Jesus-Messiah-shaped faith that functioned both as the sacrifice and the apostolate. This is what the Jesus-Messiah festival looked like. If Paul were called to face martyrdom right then and there, his death would be like the drink offering, the libation, poured out on top of the sacrifice, which should simply increase the level of celebration. The unrestrained nature of Paul's metaphor reflects the extravagant way in which he had taken the most central event of daily, weekly, and annual pagan religion and made it serve the cause of Jesus-Messiah.

In Paul's Epistle to the Philippians, he repeatedly called for the unity and solidarity of the church. *Sacrifice* was part of what happened when the little community, facing persecution, was learning to work out its own salvation. They must realize—not least at times of festival and sacrifice—that

God himself is the one who was at work among them. Paul was still working with the assumption that religion is what strengthens and unites the city state—with the difference that the city state in question consisted of Jesus-Messiah's people, those whose citizenship is in heaven, against the day when heaven and earth are brought together at last. He thanked the Philippians for the gift they had sent him. It was like a sacrifice with a beautiful smell, a worthy offering, giving pleasure. This was the emphatically Christian version of the religion by which the sacrifices of the community in the Roman world would have helped to strengthen the bonds, both human and divine, that held them together. His Second Epistle to the Corinthians also indicates the same stitching together of divine and human gifts for the good of the community.

Paul does not always allude to pagan festivities but to the regular joyful procession of Jews from the far-off lands of the Diaspora, coming together to Jerusalem for the great Jewish festivals. Paul was transforming Jewish religion and emphasized the moment of covenant renewal promise in Deuteronomy 30. If in Philippians 2 he were to be the libation on the sacrifice, here the gentile Christians were the sacrifice and he was the priest who was presenting them at the altar. Therefore, Paul had not focused on Jerusalem as the center of the earth. The basic movement of his mission was centrifugal not centripetal, that is, to the wider world of the gentiles. And Paul's proclamation bears repeating: "For I am not ashamed of the gospel, because it is the power of God that brings salvation to everyone who believes: *first to the Jew, then to the Gentile*" (Rom 1:16, my emphasis).

This is religion reborn. Paul rejected everything about pagan religion. But Christian religion itself—centered upon the celebration that offered a sacrifice, through which humans and the Triune God are bound together in the solidarity of one community and its consequent fruitfulness—was something now fulfilled and transformed in and through Jesus-Messiah. Pagan religion was a parody of it and Judaism pointed to it. Now we have the final exodus, the new temple, the true sacrifice, the new priesthood, the libation poured out on top of the celebratory sacrifice—Israel transformed and fulfilled in Jesus-Messiah.

Chapter 6

Paul's Mysticism of the New Creation

"Therefore, if anyone is in Christ, the new creation has come:
The old has gone, the new is here!" (2 Cor 5:17)

Rethinking Heaven

"But our citizenship is in heaven. And we eagerly await
a Savior from there, the Lord Jesus Christ." (Phil 3:20)

THIS FINAL CHAPTER FOCUSES on two aspects of Paul's worldview: that
of heaven, which contradicts much of present-day Christian thinking
on this matter, and his mysticism of the new creation. Is not the popular
view of afterlife that of an ethereal heaven devoid of everything we know
on earth except God, angels, and an almost disembodied communion of
saints? Heaven is actually a reverent way of speaking about God. Biblical
heaven is not a future destiny but the other, hidden dimension of ordinary
life—God's transcendent dimension. Biblically speaking, the word *heaven*
is a figure of speech that designates God's dwelling place. However, it is
used more often as a metaphor for the fullness of salvation enjoyed by
those who are finally saved in God. It expresses God's sovereignty over
everything and the quality of eternal life. The sixth-century Roman philosopher Boethius penned what some consider the classic definition of
eternal life: the simultaneous and perfect possession of never-ending *life*.[1]
More to the main point: the kingdom of *heaven* is the glorious *transforma-*
tion of *all creation* into a *new heaven and a new earth.* Thy kingdom come
on earth as it is in heaven. The Bible's last book, Revelation, does *not* focus
on saved souls making their way to a disembodied heaven, but rather on

---

1. Boethius, *De consol. phil.,* 5, pr. 6:4.

the New Jerusalem coming *down from heaven* to *earth* that brings about the *new heaven and the new earth.*[2]

Such a belief also underscores what one finds in the Bible's first book, Genesis: God creating everything good, which God will *transform* in the age to come as the new creation. As a result, "riches in heaven" simply refers to riches kept in God's presence. One might also think of it as the place (which it is not) where God's purposes for the future are stored up—where they are kept safe until the day when they become a reality *on earth*. When Paul wrote that "we know that if the earthly tent we live in is destroyed, we have a building from God, an eternal house in heaven, not built by human hands. Meanwhile we groan, longing to be clothed instead with our heavenly dwelling, because when we are clothed, we will not be found naked. For while we are in this tent, we groan and are burdened, because we do not wish to be unclothed but to be clothed instead with our heavenly dwelling, so that what is mortal may be swallowed up by life" (2 Cor 5:1–4). Paul was referring to the incorruptible new creation and the transformed physical body that is in some sense already present in heaven so that it can be brought to birth in the new creation, the renewed world. Christians must realize that heaven means "God's space," that earth means "our space," and that these two, made from the start to overlap and interlock, did so fully and finally in Jesus. Heaven and earth are already joined in Jesus-Messiah's glorified and ascended body, now fully and thoroughly at home in heaven. And they were joined again, in the opposite direction, as it were, when the powerful wind of the Holy Spirit came upon the disciples, just as the presence of God filled the tabernacle and Solomon's Temple with divine glory. With Jesus-Messiah and the Holy Spirit, the new creation has already come into being.

The first Christians and Paul did not simply believe in life after death. They almost never spoke of going to heaven when they died. They did speak of "being with the Lord" as their destination after death, but regarded it as a temporary stage on the way to eventual bodily resurrection. However, late medieval theology moved away from this biblical view to identify salvation and the ultimate promised future, not as a new creation, but as "going permanently home to heaven." Moreover, this was understood as an almost Platonic, disembodied, ethereal realm, with only minimal attention to the biblical meaning of bodily resurrection. Thus, it is not surprising that when Christians are asked what is life's goal, most will reply: to save my soul, go to heaven, and to see God eternally.

2. Isaiah also prophesied: "See, I will create new heavens and a new earth" (Isa 65:17).

The apostle Paul declared: "then we shall see face to face" (1 Cor 13:12).[3] Therefore, heaven was sometimes described as a place where a person will have the beatific vision, popularly understood as some sort of celestial and ethereal seeing of God on a giant, flat-screen TV—a caricature, but not much of one. One finds in Christian history many thinkers who understood the beatific vision as a prolonged form of monotony. Descartes feared the boredom that would arise from contemplating God eternally. Amusingly, the twentieth-century French journalist André Frossard quipped that Descartes did not have the clear and distinct idea that perhaps God might get bored much more quickly with contemplating Descartes. Correctly understood, however, the beatific vision emphasized the *complete fulfillment* of the human being as an individual and as a social and earthly being. On the basis of Revelation 22:3–5, the light of glory is required to see God and all else in God. The Lord God will be the *light* in which and through which everything is seen.

Even many contemporary Christians misunderstand Paul's text, which states: "But our citizenship is in heaven. And we eagerly await a Savior from there, the Lord Jesus Christ, who, by the power that enables him to bring everything under his control, will transform our lowly bodies so that they will be like his glorious body" (Phil 3:20–21). Many Christians erroneously suppose that being citizens of heaven means looking forward to the time when they will live there forever. Even the direct statement about a Savior *from there* who will transform our lowly bodies into Jesus-Messiah's "glorious body" is misconstrued as actually affirming that they will be "going permanently home to heaven."[4]

However, Paul's idea about citizenship did not center on a place of residence but on status and allegiance. Rome had created colonies, not only to extend its influence around the Mediterranean world, but also to prevent retired solders with blood and time on their hands from being in Rome and ready to cause trouble. Those granted citizenship in the imperial cities would *not* have interpreted it as an invitation to retire to Rome. Moreover, in times of crisis, the Roman Emperor would *come* to deliver them from any local difficulties they were having.

What Paul meant was that the Savior, the Lord, Jesus the King—all imperial titles, which in this context, were blatantly counter-imperial—will

3. Also see Exod 33:17–33; Matt 5:8; John 14:8; 1 John 3:2. However, see 1 Tim 6:15–16, "God, whom no one has seen or can see."

4. Wright, *Resurrection*, 229–36.

come *from heaven* to change the present condition of his people. The key word is *transform*. Jesus-Messiah will transform our current "lowly" present body to be like his "glorious body." What underlies this view is a theology of creation. Though this text focuses mainly on human resurrection, "transformed physicality" (N. T. Wright), it indicates that this will take place through God's victorious transformation of the entire cosmos. Thus, when Paul wrote of heavenly citizenship, he was not looking forward to going to heaven to be there permanently, but to the time when Jesus-Messiah would come *from heaven* to change Paul's present body into a glorious body like Jesus-Messiah's own.

The Torah, the Prophets, the Psalms, and Paul expressed Israel's hope in a variety of ways. Salvation for the Jews, and therefore for Paul, did not call for a freeing action that would snatch Israel or the faithful from the world, but for a freeing that would be *for this world*, and for the role for which humans were created. It was the hoped-for renewed world in which justice and mercy would reign forever. There was a radical redefinition of the Jewish hope of liberation from pagan oppression, real justice, and peace for the world when God ultimately returned to his temple. In Paul's view, redemption did not mean "going permanently home to heaven," but that the kingdom of God would come on earth as it is in heaven. He would have definitely agreed with what was written in 2 Peter 3:13: "But in keeping with his promise we are looking forward to a new heaven and a new earth, where righteousness dwells."

A misreading of Paul's 2 Corinthians also caused and still causes some Christians to think that salvation is all about "going permanently home to heaven." Paul wrote: "For we know that if the earthly tent we live in is destroyed, we have a building from God, an eternal house in heaven, not built by human hands. Meanwhile we groan, longing to be clothed instead with our heavenly dwelling, because when we are clothed, we will not be found naked. For while we are in this tent, we groan and are burdened, because we do not wish to be unclothed but to be clothed instead with our heavenly dwelling, so that what is mortal may be swallowed up by life" (2 Cor 5:1–4).

In this text, Paul wrote about a new tent, or building, or house, or body awaiting us within God's realm—again, heaven—ready for us to put on over the present one so that what is mortal may be swallowed up with eternal life. Of course, Paul insisted that this will be accomplished through the Holy Spirit. Modern Westerners take for granted a basic ontological contrast between *spirit*, in the sense of something immaterial, and *matter*, in the sense of something material and physical. They assume that the only way to be permanent and immortal is to become nonphysical.

However, Jewish creation theology, reinforced by Jesus' bodily resurrection, gave rise to Paul's mystical view of the new creation. Did he not write later in this chapter, "if anyone is in Christ, the new creation has come" (2 Cor 5:17)? Paul focused on a new type of physicality, which stands in relation to our present body as our current body does to a wraith. The transformed physicality of Jesus-Messiah's body means that our future, glorious bodies will be far *more* substantial—more *bodily*—than our existing one. Just as a seriously ill person is often only a "shadow" of his or her former self, so is the existing body in contrast to the body stored "in heaven." If guests are assured that choice wine is kept in a wine cellar, this does not mean that they will have to go into the wine cellar to enjoy it with a meal. The host will get the wine. Despite Paul's somewhat awkward metaphor, his emphasis was really on transformed physicality—to be clothed with immortality by the Holy Spirit, when one is resurrected from the dead, as was Jesus-Messiah.

Two other texts that lend themselves to misinterpretation are:

> For to me, to live is Christ and to die is gain. If I am to go on living in the body, this will mean fruitful labor for me. Yet what shall I choose? I do not know! I am torn between the two: I desire to depart and be with Christ, which is better by far; but it is more necessary for you that I remain in the body. (Phil 1:21–24)

and

> Therefore we are always confident and know that as long as we are at home in the body we are away from the Lord. For we live by faith, not by sight. We are confident, I say, and would prefer to be away from the body and at home with the Lord. So we make it our goal to please him, whether we are at home in the body or away from it. (2 Cor 5: 6–9)

In these texts, Paul was emphasizing his personal knowledge of and intimate relationship with Jesus-Messiah, for which he considered everything else as "dung." These texts reflect back on the present, explaining why, in the light of this future, one should have confidence and do work pleasing to the Lord. It anticipates Paul's further explanation of the nature of his apostolic ministry of reconciliation in 2 Corinthians 5:11—6:13. Paul still expected the return of Jesus, and with it the resurrection of the dead. In 1 Corinthians 15:51 ("We will not all sleep, but we will all be changed"), we see Paul assuming that he would be among those still alive at that time. However, he was now facing the prospect that he might well die before it all happened. This, he anticipated, when he wrote:

> I eagerly expect and hope that I will in no way be ashamed, but will have sufficient courage so that now as always Christ will be exalted in my body, whether by life or by death. For to me, to live is Christ and to die is gain. If I am to go on living in the body, this will mean fruitful labor for me. Yet what shall I choose? I do not know! I am torn between the two: I desire to depart and be with Christ, which is better by far; but it is more necessary for you that I remain in the body. (Phil 1: 20–24)

The perils of his apostolate had also caused him to confess that he once "despaired of life itself" (2 Cor 1:8). Thus, Paul's emphasis on Jesus' bodily resurrection as the prototype of our future glorious resurrected body refutes the non-Christian view that in the end Christians will go to join Jesus-Messiah in a non-bodily, Platonic heaven. God created humans for this world, which will be gloriously reaffirmed in God's eventual future. Belief in the bodily resurrection includes the belief that what is done in the present in the body, by the power of the Holy Spirit, will be affirmed in the eventual future in ways in which we can only presently guess.

A Mysticism of the New Creation

In their reading of Paul, a number of contemporary scholars have asked what relationship exists between the wider natural world, the world of galaxies and stars, mountains and seas, bacteria, plants, and animals, etc., and the life, death, and resurrection of Jesus Christ? While in the Christian East the threefold interrelationship between God, human beings, and the wider creation, found in the scriptures and patristic writers had been maintained, the wider creation had been largely dropped in the West. In short, the theological meaning of mountains, seas, animals, plants, the climate of our planet, the Milky Way galaxy, and the observable and non-observable universe involves the entire story of God's self-communication, not only to human beings, but also to all creatures through creation, incarnation, and final transfiguration. Thus, because of the biblical promises of a new heavens and a new earth, salvation can be seen to involve the *whole* creation.[5]

In 2 Corinthians 5:17, Paul emphasized not heaven but: "if anyone is in Christ, the new creation has come: The old has gone, the new is here!" Thus, the risen Christ as the "new creation" is the real, present anticipation (*proleptic*, in technical terms) of the new Jerusalem, *coming down out of heaven* from God whose dwelling place is now among the people with whom he will dwell and will make all things new (Rev 21:2–5). This conviction signifies the new heaven and the new earth, a *cosmic* resurrection in which God will be all in all (1 Cor 15: 28). As common as it is to think of the afterlife in immaterial terms, this view ignores that we are saved not as souls but as whole persons, social and cosmic resurrected body-persons, not in an ethereal heaven but as part of the new heaven *and the new earth.*

Paul also connected his mysticism of the new creation to his mysticism of the cross when he wrote: "But may it never be that I would boast, except in the cross of our Lord Jesus Christ, through which the world has been crucified to me, and I to the world. For neither is circumcision anything, nor uncircumcision, but a new creation. And those who will walk by this rule, peace and mercy be upon them, and upon the Israel of God" (Gal 6:14–16). Paul emphasized that "a person is not a Jew who is one only outwardly, nor is circumcision merely outward and physical. No, a person is a Jew who is one inwardly; and circumcision is circumcision of the heart, by the Spirit, not by the written code" (Rom 2:28–29). Often overlooked is the fact that the "Israel of God" means the entirety of Jesus-Messiah's people, be they Jewish or non-Jewish. The death of Jesus as Israel's Messiah was the means by which the power of the old world was abolished and that by which those who belong to Jesus-Messiah became part of the new creation. The new creation determined the identity of the single-family, the seed promised to Abraham, and in so doing destroyed the distinctions arising from the marks of circumcision or gentile pride and uncircumcision. Israel now denoted the entire faith-family of Jesus-Messiah, defined by faith working through love and new creation.

N. T. Wright considers Romans 8:18–28 to be "one of the most central statements in the New Testament about what God intends to do with the whole cosmos." He further contends that: "[t]his is not, then, a theology in which human beings are set free from space-time existence and escape into

---

5. Lohfink, *Is This All There Is?* 184–93.

a 'salvation' which is detached from the created world."[6] Wright criticizes what he describes as an escapist salvation, the notion that, as humans, we must leave the cosmos to its own devices and find salvation in the pure realm of the spirit. In his view, this erroneous perspective frequently influences the way Christians conceive of the afterlife as something purely ethereal. Paul is remarkably close to a Jewish apocalyptic perspective when he proposes that the corruption and redemption of creation are central concepts in the theology of numerous Jewish apocalyptic writings.

To understand Paul's mysticism of the new creation, one must focus on the concise formulation in Romans 8:19–23:

> For the creation waits in eager expectation for the children of God to be revealed. For the creation was subjected to frustration, not by its own choice, but by the will of the one who subjected it, in hope that the creation itself will be liberated from its bondage to decay and brought into the freedom and glory of the children of God. We know that the whole creation has been groaning as in the pains of childbirth right up to the present time. Not only so, but we ourselves, who have the first fruits of the Spirit, groan inwardly as we wait eagerly for our adoption to sonship, the redemption of our bodies.

Hence, all creation groans because of the sin of our proto-parents, Adam and Eve. Just as sin affected everything, the risen Christ is the seed of the transformed creation. Paul's creation-theology text concentrates not only on the whole of human creation but also on the nonhuman world subjected to futility and still awaiting to be set free from bondage. The promises in Romans 8 for the future of the material universe is unquestionably apocalyptic. The bodily resurrection of Jesus-Messiah should remind Christians that they have already begun to experience the new creation and that they must still pass through a period of suffering and hardship before final glory. Even though Paul referred briefly to cosmic redemption, his principal purpose was to focus on Christian believers, who were experiencing suffering. Still, this does not mean that there is no reference to a transformation of the cosmos. Romans 8 stressed the intermediate time between becoming a Christian and the full completion of the transformation initiated, which must include a time of present suffering. What he wrote in 2 Corinthians 4:17 is consonant with this, namely, "[f]or our light and momentary troubles are achieving for us an eternal glory that far outweighs them all."

6. Wright, *New Heavens, New Earth*, 12–13.

Based on solid exegetical grounding, Michael Fahey, a friend and colleague, wrote a helpful free paraphrase of Romans 8. It reads:

> To speak metaphorically, the entire material universe, earth and the whole cosmos, exists in an anxious state of anticipation as it awaits the next stage in the transformation of human beings. In the past, nonhuman creation on earth was cursed by God [as a result of the fall of Adam and Eve] to an ignominious state [fields required tilling, climate presented challenges, unpredictable problems caused men to labor by the sweat of their brows]. The universe is hoping to share the same kind of freedom, a newness that has already begun in those humans transformed in Christ. Right up to today, the material universe is, so to speak, groaning in unison, experiencing, so to speak, the pangs of childbirth. But not only the material universe is awaiting this full transformation into a new creation but we Christians also, who already have received the Holy Spirit through faith and baptism, are still groaning inwardly, awaiting expectantly our complete transformation at our resurrection in the world to come.

This passage in Romans distinguished clearly two aspects of creation, which in verse 19 refers to nonhuman creation (i.e., "nature" as a whole). First, it is poetically imagined as longing for a future event. This is the creation subjected to frustration, the very same creation hoping to be set free (again metaphorically) from its bondage to decay. This is the whole creation said to be groaning and suffering the pangs of childbirth. Second, Paul then went on to assert that not only earthly material creation, but also we ourselves are a special form of creation because we have received the first fruits of the Holy Spirit and are groaning inwardly and eagerly awaiting a perfected form of redemption. This echoes the same sort of dialectical paradox found in the Gospels when Jesus spoke of God's kingdom as something already here but not yet fully realized.

Jewish apocalyptic held the view that the fall of Adam corrupted the world, and that the world's perfection will come through a decisive divine intervention. Enoch's midrash exposition of the flood story includes reference to ideas also found in the text of Romans 8, namely creation's enslavement to meaninglessness; creation groaning because it is under oppression (in 1 Enoch assigned to the malevolence of the fallen angels and the giants); the expectation that the sons of God will be revealed; and that creation itself will attain freedom. What is distinctive about this passage in Romans is that Christian believers are already God's children, and hence part of the family of Jesus-Messiah. Thus, they are gradually being formed into Jesus-Messiah's likeness and will share eschatological glory together with him.

Again in 2 Cor 5:17 Paul emphasized new creation, his ministry, and reconciliation: "Therefore, if anyone is in Christ, the new creation has come: The old has gone, the new is here! All this is from God, who reconciled us to himself through Christ and gave us the ministry of reconciliation: that God was reconciling the world to himself in Christ, not counting people's sins against them. And he has committed to us the message of reconciliation. We are therefore Christ's ambassadors, as though God were making his appeal through us. We implore you on Christ's behalf: Be reconciled to God." Paul further highlighted his main points this way:

> The Son is the image of the invisible God, the firstborn over all creation. For in him all things were created: things in heaven and on earth, visible and invisible, whether thrones or powers or rulers or authorities; all things have been created through him and for him. He is before all things, and in him all things hold together. And he is the head of the body, the church; he is the beginning and the firstborn from among the dead, so that in everything he might have the supremacy. For God was pleased to have all his fullness dwell in him, and through him to reconcile to himself all things, whether things on earth or things in heaven, by making peace through his blood, shed on the cross. (Col 1:15–20)

As a result, Paul, by proclaiming that in Jesus-Messiah God was reconciling the cosmos to himself, saw reconciliation as cosmic. To be sure, Paul stressed mainly the reconciliation of humanity because cosmic creation cannot be accomplished unless humanity is first reconciled. But for Paul, while God's purpose in reconciliation is *initially* directed at humanity, it does not *end* with humanity since it embraces "all things, whether things on earth or in heaven." Besides, this text also stresses Jesus-Messiah not only as the firstborn from the dead but also as the firstborn of all creation.

The principal interest in a renovated created universe relates to the status of the setting for our resurrected bodies. If there is a resurrection after death, then there has to be some material setting in which this body can be situated. The resurrected body will be incorruptible, transformed physicality and not immaterial. John Polkinhorne, the English theoretical physicist, theologian, and Anglican priest, wrote that even if there will occur a "death" of the cosmos as we know it, the cosmos also can experience a resurrection. "The resurrection of Jesus is the seminal event from which the whole of God's new creation has already begun to grow."[7] Just as we expect our bodies by their resurrection to be transformed so too will it be with the non-human creation. Of course, the transmuted "matter" of the new creation will be the setting for human re-embodiment in the resurrection life. Polkinghorne further reasons (unconvincingly to my mind) that there will be time in eternity, a temporal setting whose character is everlasting.

Unfortunately many Christians have interpreted apocalyptic passages in the New Testament, such as Matthew 24:29 ("immediately after the tribulation of those days the sun will be darkened, and the moon will not give its light, and the stars will fall from heaven, and the powers of the heavens will be shaken"; see also Mark 13:24–27), as *literal* prophecies about the annihilation or extinction of the universe. Such Christians have failed to recognize these Gospel apocalyptic discourses as a literary genre whose primary purpose was meant to predict not the annihilation of the universe but rather more immediately the destruction of Jerusalem in the first century, a view convincingly defended in the many works of N. T. Wright.

Paul referred at least obliquely to the conviction that the non-human setting or cosmos of our experience will indeed survive and be transformed into a "new," transformed creation that will endure forever. This is one of the key elements to the Christian conviction that we shall be raised in the resurrection of our mortal bodies, which the church's various creeds so aptly proclaim. It is impossible to conceive of transformed physicality, the resurrected body-person, in a way that does not include transformed matter. In short, eternal life cannot be purely spiritual because human beings are not purely spiritual. Paul understood Christians as living in the present age *and* in the age to come because the new creation has already begun. Because Jesus-Messiah is the seed of the new creation, both human beings and all creation are now part of the new creation.

Although the theme of the transformation of the material universe is not developed at length in the writings of the apostle Paul, it has a firm foundation both in the Jewish scriptures and in the later Christian tradition. The book of Genesis proclaims that God not only created everything good but also that God established a rainbow covenant with Noah, his descendants, *and every living creature on earth* (Gen 9:17). Isaiah prophesied: "See, I will create new heavens and a new earth" (Isa 65:17). Jesus was also specific: his Father does not forget even the lowly sparrow (Luke 12:6). John's Gospel proclaimed that "[t]hrough him all things were made;

7. Polkinghorne, *The God of Hope*, 113.

without him nothing was made that has been made" (John 1:3). The book of Revelation proclaimed that the lamb on the throne makes *all things* new and every creature in the new heaven and on the new earth and under the earth and in the sea, and all that is in them, sings a hymn of praise to the slain lamb (Rev 5:12).

St. Augustine is paradigmatic of the many Christian mystics who have felt, tasted, touched, smelled, and seen God with their mystical senses. He wrote:

> But what do I love when I love you? Not the beauty of body nor the gracefulness of temporal rhythm, not the brightness of light so friendly to the eyes, not the sweet and various melodies of songs, not the fragrance of flowers and ointments and spices, not manna and honey; not limbs receptive to fleshly embraces: I love not these when I love my God. And yet I do love a kind of light, melody, fragrance, food, embracement when I love my God; for He is the light, the melody, the fragrance, the food, the embracement of my inner self; Where that light shines into my soul which no place can contain, and where that voice sounds which time does not take away, and where that fragrance smells which no wind scatters, and where there is that flavor which eating does not diminish, and where there is that clinging that no satiety will separate. This is what I love when I love my God.[8]

Consonant with Paul's affirmation of the new creation, Augustine also wrote that "in heaven" we will encounter the fullness of the mystery of creation—not only God: "wherever we turn our eyes, we shall, with absolute accuracy, see God present everywhere and controlling all things, even material ones, through the bodies we shall have and through those we shall see."[9] Thus, I maintain that in the age to come, in the *new creation*, we shall not only savor the Triune God with our mystical senses but also experience *all creation* with our glorified mystical, spiritual, and *bodily* senses—sheer joy, complete happiness, and eternal love. Earlier church fathers, such as Irenaeus and Athanasius, had also written about the connection between Jesus-Messiah's cross and resurrection and the final transformation of all creation.[10] The great theologian, Maximus the Confessor, understood Jesus-Messiah as the microcosm of the entire creation, which influenced the thinking of Hans Urs von Balthasar on cosmic resurrection.

8. *Augustine of Hippo, Confessions*, bk 10, no, 6, 126.

9. Augustine, *De Civ. Dei XXII*, 29.

10. Edwards, *Deep Incarnation*, chs. 2 and 3 on the views of Irenaeus and Athanasius.

Among other authors, the seventh-century monk Julian of Toledo summed up Western patristic thought on this issue this way: "the world, having been renewed for the better, will be suitably accommodated to humans who will also have been renewed for the better in the *flesh*."[11] Likewise, the twelfth-century theologian-mystic Hugh of St. Victor established a clear connection between final resurrection and the renewal of all creation, that the world will be transformed according to the model of the resurrection.[12] Thomas Aquinas wrote that in the age to come, "the whole of bodily creation will be appropriately changed to be in harmony with the state of those resurrected."[13] The fourteenth-century Dominican mystic, Henry Suso, complained that his sins kept him from praising God. "Dear Lord," he prayed, "the frogs in the ditches praise you. And if they can't sing, at least they croak." God assured him that "there was never a creature so small or so great, so good or so bad, nor will there ever be one, that did not praise or show that I am worthy of praise."[14] And because Jesus-Messiah has been raised from the dead, this belief will be also be true in the new heaven and the new earth.

The concluding contemplation in St. Ignatius of Loyola's *Spiritual Exercises* is the "Contemplation to Obtain Divine Love." He would have persons ponder the heavens, the sun, the moon, the stars, the elements, the fruits, the birds, fish, and animals and to inform them that all creation intercedes and prays for them. This contemplation focuses on all creation as a theophany. Of course, rejoicing in creation as a theophany—a perspective as old as the psalms. St. Francis of Assisi's Canticle of Brother Sun is another paean to the interconnection of all creation as a single theophany.

The Second Vatican Council paid special attention to the cosmic side of the age to come. The *Lumen gentium* document states: "the church will receive perfection only in the glory of heaven, when the time of the renewal of all things arrives."[15] "Then, together with the human race, the universe itself, which is so closely related to man and which attains its destiny in him, will be perfectly re-established in Christ."[16] This will not take place, the

11. Julian of Toledo, *Prognosticon futuri saeculi*, 2:46.

12. Hugh of St. Victor, *De sacramentis II*, 18:1.

13. Thomas Aquinas, *IV C. Gent.*, 97.

14. *Suso, Eternal Wisdom*, ch. 24, 287.

15. Acts 3:21.

16. *LG* 48A and refers to Eph 1:10; Col 1:20; 2 Pet 3:10–13.

same document continued, "until there be realized the new heavens and a new earth where justice dwells."[17]

In Vatican II's Council Constitution of the Church in the World, *Gaudium et spes*, we read:

> the form of the world, distorted by sin, is passing away and God is preparing a new earth in which righteousness dwells, whose happiness will fill and surpass all the desires of peace arising in human hearts. Then, with death conquered, the sons and daughters of God will be raised in Christ. Love and its works will remain and all creation, which God made for us, will be set free from its bondage to decay.[18]

The Catechism of the Catholic Church also deals with the topic at length. "The visible universe is itself destined to be transformed," it declares, "so that the world itself, restored to its original state, facing no further obstacles, should be at the service of the just sharing their glorification in the risen Jesus Christ."[19] I suggest that a *Christified* universe far transcends its "original state."

Pope Francis' recent encyclical, *Laudato Si'* (no. 66), consonant with Paul's mysticism of the new creation, wrote that human life is grounded in fundamental and closely intertwined relationships: with God, with our neighbor, and with the earth. Few people remain unmoved by the stirring YouTube videos of the intimate interaction between human beings, domesticated and wild animals, and nature in all its splendor. Further, in the encyclical (nos. 83–84), we read: "The ultimate destiny of the universe is in the fullness of God, which has already been attained by the risen Christ, the measure of the maturity of all things. All creatures are moving forward with us and through us towards God. In that fullness of life and love, the risen Christ embraces and illumines all things. Human beings, endowed with intelligence and love, and drawn by the fullness of Christ, are called to lead all creatures back to their creator." Therefore, one should contemplate the entire universe as bursting with God's love and his boundless affection for us. Everything is, as it were, a caress of God. The history of our friendship with God is always linked to particular people, places, animals, rivers, mountains,

---

17. *LG 48C* and refers to 2 Pet 3:13.

18. *GS* 39A. Citing: 1 Cor 7:31; 2 Cor 5:2; 2 Pet 3:13; 1 Cor 2:9; Rev 21:4–5; 1 Cor 13:8; Rom 8: 19–21.

19. *CCC* 1042–50, esp. 1047.

oceans, natural phenomena, and so on. It is instructive that we humans share much DNA with other animals, plants, and micro-organisms.

Partially dependent on Paul, contemporary theologians write of "deep incarnation" (Niels Gregersen) and "deep resurrection" (Elizabeth Johnson). They emphasize the relationship of Jesus-Messiah's' life, death, and bodily resurrection, not only to human beings, but also to the entire observable and non-observable universe—from viruses, to black holes, galaxies, and the like. Deep incarnation and deep resurrection theology centers on Jesus-Messiah's cosmic incarnation furthered in his cosmic bodily resurrection, as the self-expression of God's Wisdom, immersed in every dimension of creation with special attention to the experiences of pain common to all sensitive creatures during the evolutionary process.

Karl Rahner emphasized that "everything has become different in the true and decisive depths of all things. [Jesus-Messiah's] resurrection is like the first eruption of a volcano, which shows that in the interior of the world God's fire is already burning, and this will bring everything to blessed ardor in his light. . . . Already from the heart of the world into which he descended in death, the new forces of a transfigured earth are at work. Already in the innermost center of all reality, futility, sin, and death are vanquished."[20] In Christ's resurrection, therefore, God has shown that he has taken all creation to himself. There is no abyss between God and world.

When asked what it all means, I point to Paul's letters and to the Book of Revelation. They taught that Jesus, the Messiah-King-Lamb, who sits at the Father's right hand, makes all things new and that every creature in the new heaven and on the new earth and under the earth and in the sea, and all that is in them, shall praise and worship the slain Lamb. Jesus, King of kings and Lord of lords, is not only the Lord-King of humans and angels, but also of animals, insects, vegetation, rivers, oceans, the sun, the moon, the planets, galaxies—the Lord-King also of the entire future new earth and new heaven. Thy kingdom come *on earth* as it is in heaven.

20. Rahner, "A Faith That Loves the Earth," 80–81.

Bibliography

Augustine. *Augustine of Hippo—Selected Writings, The Confessions*. Translated by Mary T. Clark. New York: Paulist, 1984.

Aulén, Gustav. *Christus Victor: Three Mains Types of the Idea of Atonement*. Translated by A. G. Hebert. Reprint, Eugene, OR: Wifp & Stock, 2003.

Barth, Karl. *Epistle to the Romans*. Translated by Edwyn C. Hoskins. Oxford: Oxford University Press, 1975.

———. *Die Kirchliche Dogmatik*. Zürich: Theologischer Verlag, 1993.

Bauckham, Richard. *God Crucified: Monotheism and Christology in the New Testament*. Didsbury Lectures. Carlisle, UK: Paternoster, 1999.

———. *Jesus and the God of Israel: God Crucified and Other Studies on the New Testament's Christology of Divine Identity*. Milton Keynes, UK: Paternoster, 2008.

Boccaccini, Gabriele, and Carlos A. Segovia, eds. *Paul the Jew: Rereading the Apostle as a Figure of Second Temple Judaism*. Minneapolis: Fortress, 2016.

Bouyer, Louis. "Mysticism: An Essay on the History of the Word." In *Understanding Mysticism*, edited by Richard Woods, O.P., 42–55. Garden City, NY: Doubleday Image, 1980.

Brown, Raymond. "Does the New Testament Call Jesus God." *Theological Studies* 26.4 (1965) 545–73.

Brunner, Emil. *The Divine Imperative*. Translated by Olive Wyon. London: Lutterworth, 1937.

———. *Man in Revolt*. Translated by Olive Wyon. London: Lutterworth, 1957.

Buber, Martin, *Between Man and Man*. New York: Macmillan, 1972.

Bucke, Richard Maurice. *Cosmic Consciousness: A Study in the Evolution of the Human Mind*. Mineola, NY: Dover, 2010.

Bultmann, Rudolf. *The Gospel of John*. Philadelphia: Westminster, 1971.

———. *Theologie des Neuen Testaments*. 6th ed. Tübingen: Mohr, 1968.

Chardin, Pierre Teilhard de. *The Divine Milieu*. Translated by Sion Cowell. New York: Harper, 1968.

———. *Human Energy*. Translated by J. M. Cohen. New York: Harcourt Brace Jonanovich, 1969.

———. *Let Me Explain*. Edited by Jean Pierre Dumoulin; translated by René Hague. New York: Harper & Row, 1970.

Dumoulin, Jean Pierre, ed. *Let Me Explain*. New York: Harper & Row, 1970.

Dunn, James D. G., ed. *The Cambridge Companion to St. Paul*. Cambridge: Cambridge University Press, 2003.

Dunn, James D. G., and Maurice Wiles. "M. Wiles on *Christology in the Making* and Responses by the Author." In James D. G. Dunn, *The Christ and the Spirit, Volume 1: Christology*, 257–69. Grand Rapids: Eerdmans, 1998.

Edwards, Denis. *Deep Incarnation*. Maryknoll, NY: Orbis, 2019.

Egan, Harvey D. "Christian Mysticism and Psychedelic Drugs." *Studies in Formative Spirituality* V.1 (1984) 33–41.

———. *Christian Mysticism: The Future of a Tradition*. New York: Pueblo, 1984.

———. "Evelyn Underhill Revisited." *The Way* 51.1 (2012) 223–39.

———. *Soundings in the Christian Mystical Tradition*. Collegeville, MN: Liturgical, 2010.

Fremantle, Anne. *The Protestant Mystics*. Boston: Little, Brown, 1964.

Gregory of Nyssa, *The Great Catechism*. New York: Christian Literature Publishing, 1892 & Aeterna, 2016.

———. *Life of Moses*, trans. Abraham Malherbe and Everett Ferguson. New York, Paulist, 1978.

Hadewijch: The Complete Works. Trans. Mother Columba Hart. New York: Paulist, 1980.

Hill, Wesley. *Paul and the Trinity*. Grand Rapids: Eerdmans, 2015.

Hurtado, Larry W. *Destroyer of the Gods: Early Christian Distinctiveness in the Roman World*. Waco, TX: Baylor University Press, 2016.

———. *How on Earth Did Jesus Become a God? Historical Questions about Earliest Devotion to Jesus*. Grand Rapids: Eerdmans, 2005.

———. *Lord Jesus Christ: Devotion to Jesus and Earliest Christianity*. Grand Rapids: Eerdmans, 2003.

Huxley, Aldous. *The Doors of Perception*. New York: Harper & Row, 1954.

Ignatius of Loyola. *A Pilgrim's Journey: The Autobiography of Ignatius of Loyola*. Translated by Joseph N. Tylenda. Wilmington, DE: Glazier, 1985.

James, William. *The Varieties of Religious Experience*. New York: New American Library, 1958.

John of the Cross. *The Collected Works of St. John of the Cross*. Translated by Kieran Kavanaugh, OCD and Otilio Rodriguez, OCD. Washington, DC: Institute of Carmelite Studies, 1976.

Johnston, William, ed. *The Cloud of Unknowing and the Book of Privy Counseling*. Garden City, NJ: Doubleday-Image, 1976.

Julian of Norwich. *Julian of Norwich—Showings*. Translated by Edmund Colledge and James Walsh. New York: Paulist, 1978.

Lohfink, Gerhard. *Is This All There Is? On Resurrection and Eternal Life*. Translated by Linda M. Malone. Collegeville, MN: Liturgical, 2018.

Lonergan, Bernard. *Method in Theology*. London: Darton, Longman & Todd, 1972.

Lubac, Henri de. *Corpus Mysticum: The Eucharist and the Church in the Middles Ages*. Translated by Gemma Simmonds, CJ, with Richard Price and Christopher Stephens; edited by Laurence Paul Hemming and Susan Frank Parsons. Notre Dame, IN: University of Notre Dame Press, 2006.

Marie of the Incarnation. *Marie of the Incarnation: Selected Writings*. Edited and translated by Irene Mahoney, OSU. New York: Paulist, 1989.

Marxsen, Willi. *The Resurrection of Jesus of Nazareth*. Translated by Margaret Kohl. Philadelphia: Fortress, 1968.

Matthiessen, Peter. "A Reporter at Large: The Snow Leopard I." *New Yorker*, March 27, 1978.

McCabe, Herbert. *God Still Matters*. Edited by Brian Davies. London: Continuum, 2002.

McGinn, Bernard. *The Essential Writings of Christian Mysticism*. New York: The Modern Library, 2006.

———. *The Foundations of Mysticism: Origins to the Fifth Century. The Presence of God: A History of Western Christian Mysticism* I. New York: Crossroad, 1991.

———. *Mysticism in the Reformation (1500–1650). The Presence of God: A History of Western Christian Mysticism* VI.1. New York: Crossroad, 2016.

———. *The Persistence of Mysticism and Catholic Europe: France, Italy, and Germany (1500–1675). The Presence of God: A History of Western Christian Mysticism* VI. New York: Crossroad, 2020.

———. *The Varieties of Vernacular Mysticism 1350–1550. The Presence of God: A History of Western Christian Mysticism* V. New York: Crossroad, 2012.

McGrath, James F. *The Only True God: Early Christian Monotheism in Its Jewish Context*. Urbana, IL: University of Illinois Press, 2009.

Merton, Thomas. "First Christmas at Gethsemane." *Catholic World* 170 (December 1949) 166–73.

Metz, Johann Baptist. *Faith in History and Society: Toward a Practical Fundamental Theology*. Translated by J. Matthew Ashley. New York: Crossroad, 2013.

Moltmann, Jürgen. *The Crucified God: The Cross of Christ as the Foundation and Criticism of Christian Theology*. Minneapolis: Fortress, 2015.

O'Collins, Gerald. *Believing in the Resurrection: The Meaning and Promise of the Risen Christ*. New York: Paulist, 2012.

Pitstick, Lyra. *Christ's Descent into Hell: John Paul II, Joseph Ratzinger, and Hans Urs von Balthasar on the Theology of Holy Saturday*. Grand Rapids: Eerdmans, 2016.

———. *Light in Darkness: Hans Urs von Balthasar and the Catholic Doctrine of Christ's Descent into Hell*. Grand Rapids: Eerdmans, 2007.

Plato. *The Republic*. Translated by G. M. A. Grube. Indianapolis: Hackett, 1974.

Polkinghorne, John. *The God of Hope and the End of the World*. New Haven, CT: Yale University Press, 2002.

Raguin, Yves. *The Depth of God*. St. Meinrad, IN: Abbey, 1975.

Rahner, Hugo. *The Vision of St. Ignatius in the Chapel of La Storta*. Rome: Centrum Ignatianum Spiritualitatis, 1979.

Rahner, Karl. "The Eternal Significance of the Humanity of Jesus for Our Relation with God." In Karl Rahner, *Theological Investigations III*, translated by Karl-H. and Boniface Kruger, 35–46. Baltimore: Helicon, 1967.

———. "A Faith That Loves the Earth." In Karl Rahner, *Everyday Faith*, translated by W. J. O'Hara, 76–85. New York: Herder, 1968.

Richards, Hubert J. *The First Easter: What Really Happened?* Mystic, CT: Twenty-Third, 1986.

Rutledge, Fleming. *The Crucifixion: Understanding the Death of Jesus Christ*. Grand Rapids: Eerdmans, 2015.

Scholem, Gershom. *Major Trends in Jewish Mysticism*. New York: Schocken, 1954.

———. "Mysticism and Society." *Diogenes* 15.58 (1967) 1–24.

Schweitzer, Albert. *The Mysticism of Paul the Apostle*. Translated by William Montgomery. Baltimore: Johns Hopkins, 1998.

Stace, Walter T. *The Teachings of the Mystics*. New York: New American Library, 1960.

Suso, Henry. *Henry Suso: The Exemplar, with Two German Sermons, Book of Eternal Wisdom*. Translated and edited by Frank Tobin. New York: Paulist, 1989.

Underhill, Evelyn. *Mysticism: A Study in the Nature and Development of Man's Spiritual Consciousness*. New York: New American Library, 1974.

Wainwright, Arthur W. *The Trinity in the New Testament*. London: SPCK, 1962.

Wink, Walter. *Engaging the Powers: Discernment and Resistance in a World of Domination*. Minneapolis: Fortress, 2017.

———. *Naming the Powers: The Language of Power in the New Testament*. Philadelphia: Fortress, 1984.

———. *Unmasking the Powers: The Invisible Forces that Determine Human Existence*. Philadelphia: Fortress, 1986.

Winter, Paul. *On the Trial of Jesus*. Berlin: de Gruyter, 1974.

Wong, Joseph H., and Harvey D. Egan. *The Christology and Mystical Theology of Karl Rahner*. New York: Crossroad, 2020.

Wright, N. T. *The Day the Revolution Began: Reconsidering the Meaning of Jesus' Crucifixion*. New York: HarperCollins, 2016.

———. *Interpreting Jesus: Essays on the Gospels*. Grand Rapids: Zondervan Academic, 2020.

———. *New Heavens, New Earth: The Biblical Picture of Christian Hope*. Cambridge: Grove, 1999.

———. *Paul: A Biography*. New York: HarperCollins, 2008.

———. *Paul and the Faithfulness of God*. 2 vols. London: SPCK, 2013.

———. *The Resurrection of the Son of God*. London: SPCK, 2003.

Wright, N. T., and Michael F. Bird. *The New Testament in Its World*. Grand Rapids: Zondervan, 2019.